Little Farmstead Living

LITTLE FARMSTEAD
LIVING

*Creating a Country Life
Just Past the City Limits*

JULIE THOMAS

Martingale®
Create with Confidence

Little Farmstead Living:
Creating a Country Life Just Past the City Limits
© 2019 by Julie Thomas

Create with Confidence

Martingale®
19021 120th Ave. NE, Ste. 102
Bothell, WA 98011-9511 USA
ShopMartingale.com

Printed in China
24 23 22 21 20 19   8 7 6 5 4 3 2 1

Library of Congress Cataloging-in-Publication Data is
available upon request.

ISBN: 978-1-68356-014-2

CREDITS

PUBLISHER AND
CHIEF VISIONARY OFFICER
Jennifer Erbe Keltner

CONTENT DIRECTOR
Karen Costello Soltys

PRODUCTION MANAGER
Regina Girard

MANAGING EDITOR
Tina Cook

COVER AND
BOOK DESIGNER
Adrienne Smitke

COPY EDITOR
Sheila Chapman Ryan

PHOTOGRAPHERS
Adam Albright
Brent Kane

ADDITIONAL PHOTOGRAPHY

Page 142, top right: Gladwin Johnson

Page 144: Studio B Portraits (StudioBportraits.com)

Dedication

For...

*My husband, Aaron, whose love, kindness, strength,
and humor bless me daily as we walk through life together.*

*My children, Hudson, Noah, and Lincoln, who are
and will forever be my greatest dreams come true.*

*My parents, who have poured their love, support,
and prayers into the foundation of our family.*

Little Farmstead

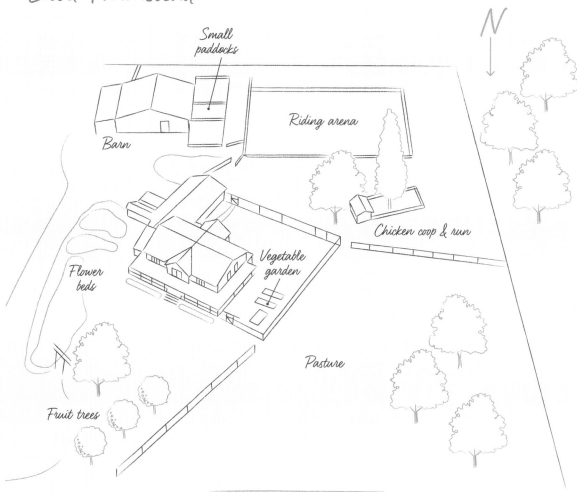

Small paddocks

N

Riding arena

Barn

Flower beds

Vegetable garden

Chicken coop & run

Pasture

Fruit trees

CONTENTS

INTRODUCTION

"Everyone has, I think, in some quiet corner of the mind, an ideal home waiting to become a reality."

PAIGE RENSE

As we drive down the simple gravel driveway, past the vine-covered arbor and farmhouse, our shoulders relax. Turning in front of the barn, we are greeted by the baaing of sheep and that one extra-social chicken who, for some reason, seems to be happily awaiting our return. The sun is shining as our three sons take off in different directions. Our oldest son takes Ford and Buster, our two Labs, out into the green pasture. The dogs explore and chase each other while our son decompresses from the day. Our middle son makes a beeline for the trampoline, and our youngest is conflicted but settles on playing soccer first, then basketball. I water the newly planted vegetable garden, alone with my thoughts—but with the soundtrack of boys and dogs playing in the background.

Perhaps it was always in my heart. A desire for country living, with nature and animals as the backdrop to everyday life. Books like *Charlotte's Web* and *Little House on the Prairie* described a farmhouse family lifestyle that appealed to me. I remember as a little girl, playing with my sister and our neighbor friends in our playhouse, assigning daily chores for our make-believe life on the prairie. I suggested that someone should be in charge of tending the hay (long weeds dried in the California sunshine) behind the playhouse, and in the next breath I volunteered for the job. Armed with a garden rake, I flipped the dry weeds, imagining a barn loft full of hay bales.

When I was about nine years old, I remember asking my mother if I could plant some vegetables. In her wisdom, she recommended I start with zucchini. Seeing that fast-growing green squash take off and spread helped my confidence grow along with

them, opening my eyes to the wonder of seeds and the small victory of harvesting one's own food. Though my childhood vegetable garden didn't produce much beyond zucchini and a stray tomato, we sure enjoyed that sweet zucchini bread, and I was so proud.

I've also had a love for animals as far back as I can remember. I'll never forget the time my parents surprised my sister and me with real chicks on Easter morning. (Little did they know what they were starting, as both my sister and I keep chickens today.) For birthdays and Christmases, I'd ask for a lop-eared rabbit, horseback-riding lessons, or simply a stuffed animal to add to my collection.

When I was 11 years old, my dreams of having a horse of my own came true. One Saturday, my Dad and I went to a local horse auction—*just for fun*. I'll never forget my heart racing as my Dad raised his hand to bid on what became *my* half-Arabian, half quarter horse mare, named Desiree. Desiree means desire. God had heard the countless prayers of a young girl and had answered, through the kindness of my father (and a very sparsely attended horse auction!). For just $100, we now owned a beautiful white (technically gray) horse valued at $5,000. Since we did not live on acreage, we quickly learned just how much the cost of keeping a horse in California (far) exceeded the initial investment. But how I enjoyed those precious years growing up with my horse.

Through college and my young adult life, country dreams were replaced with the excitement of traveling around the world for jobs in technology and aerospace. My eyes were opened to different people and cultures, history, architecture, and art. These travels gave me a deeper appreciation for interior design and for incorporating timeworn treasures, which seem to have stories to tell, into our homes.

Eventually my husband and I settled in the Seattle area, which I had never visited prior to his job offer. We were soon blessed with three of the most amazing, full-of-life boys we could ever imagine. We lived in a fairly large house on a small lot in the suburbs. As our boys grew, we began to feel that although we had not outgrown the house, we'd outgrown the yard and neighborhood. This was confirmed when a well-meaning neighbor commented with a smile, "We heard you guys out in the backyard today." I'm sure she had.

My husband and I started dreaming of a place with wide-open spaces where our three sons would have room to roam and explore. Someplace where we could sit around a campfire, and finally get that dog that our boys had been asking for. Somewhere with a country landscape, just past the city limits, where we could open our doors to family and friends. We imagined a type of property that could grow with our family, giving us more reasons to be home together. Someplace for us to circle the wagons in an increasingly fast-paced world. We talked about having some animals and planting a garden. I remember describing what we were looking for to friends as a homestead or mini farm. We soon began to call it a *little farmstead*.

CHAPTER 1

The Dream

"Hope is the thing with feathers that perches in the soul—and sings the tune without the words—and never stops at all."

EMILY DICKINSON

It was a dream of a place, yet it was so much more. It would be the setting for our lives and so many memories we would create. We were looking for a change in lifestyle for our growing family. A place to put down roots . . . and wear boots. We were searching for a countryside haven, where perhaps, just maybe, we could slow down the hands of time. And if not slow them down, at least savor the moments together, and carry them in our hearts forever. (If this special place could also afford us the privacy and freedom to go outdoors in the morning in our pajamas without getting "caught" by the neighbors, all the better.)

We began our search for a home and acreage just past—but not *too* far past—the city limits. Some people go off-grid, become full-time farmers, and even aim to be self-sustaining. While this is admirable, this was not our dream. In fact, we had a relatively small radius in which we were looking, centered on my husband's work, our children's school, and our extended family. My husband was not going to quit his day job, and we didn't want our sons to have to switch schools. We were looking for a private and natural country *feel* where we could have a little bit of land, do some gardening, and care for a small menagerie of animals. Yet we also wanted to stay close enough to the activities and community our family enjoyed. I guess we were looking for the best of both worlds.

As far as acreage, we hoped for one to five acres, preferably flat, with some trees but mostly wide-open, sun-filled spaces. That much land, we figured, would allow our children plenty of room to run and explore and would provide ample space for gardening and keeping animals but still be manageable. While we love trees, here in the Pacific Northwest evergreen trees can be very dense and reduce the natural light in a home and

"The ache for home lives
in all of us, the safe place
where we can go as we are
and not be questioned."

MAYA ANGELOU

> *"Hope lies in dreams,*
> *in imagination, and in*
> *the courage of those*
> *who dare to make*
> *dreams into reality."*
>
> JONAS SALK

on a property. We were seeking a more open, usable parcel of land, hopefully one with a variety of deciduous trees. (This was the kind of property we knew we wanted for our family. To help you focus your wish list, see "Defining Your Dream Home and Acreage" on page 17.)

We thought about the many possibilities of outbuildings, and wondered if we could find a property with a chicken coop and maybe even a barn. And for the house, we hoped to find a farmhouse with lots of natural light, a room for each of our boys, good bones, and something that we could put our family's stamp on over time.

For many years we searched. We went through a lot of open houses. My sister and I would caravan our six children on house "drive-bys," often sweetening

A favorite springtime activity is making a baseball field in the side pasture (left). Our boys (ages 10, 7, and 4) on Thanksgiving morning, one week after moving here (above).

the experience for the kids with a treat at a drive-through coffee stand. I dared anyone to find a new listing with our criteria in our area faster than we could. But the proverbial (and literal) doors always seemed to close due to possible job relocations, finances, or timing. Other times, it just didn't feel quite right. During this time of searching, I struggled because I knew I had so much to be thankful for and didn't want to be materialistic. After all, we already had a nice home on the corner of a cul-de-sac. Yet, the dream of a lifestyle change for our family was so strong, I could almost taste it. The challenge was to continue to hope, dream, and trust without becoming discouraged or discontent.

And then there was this one place my sister had seen. When I first saw pictures, I wasn't all that interested. I think the dark green laminate countertops and burgundy accent wall threw me. I couldn't get a good sense of the home or property from the online listing. My husband and I decided to ask our realtor to show us anyway. And we're so glad we did. The two-plus acre property was beautiful! There were flat, green pasture areas, with just the right amount of trees. White fencing, a chicken coop, and a really nice barn had us strongly considering it. And then

there was the farmhouse. Wider than it is deep, it had a special, welcoming layout reminiscent of times gone by. With heavy pocket doors and lots of double-hung windows, it felt like a well-built classic farmhouse. It was only about 20 years old, but had the character you'd expect to find in a much older home. There were just enough rooms for our family, and lots of natural light. We knew (OK, we hoped!) this was the one. We went home and put our house up for sale.

After several months and many open houses and showings, we sold our home and were finally able to remove the "contingent" verbiage in the offer for what would become our little farmstead. And can I tell you how glad we were that none of those other places had worked out? It was truly worth the wait. We moved in to our little farmstead the week before Thanksgiving when our children were ten, seven, and four years old. We had never taken our boys through the house or property. We had taken them through so many possible houses in the past, we wanted to wait until we had the keys in hand before we showed them their new home. What an exciting day for them as they ran through the house, picked out their bedrooms, explored the barn, climbed on rocks, and got to know the lay of the land.

As with any home, there were a few compromises. Not only were the kitchen countertops dated, but so were the bathrooms. As I write this, they still are. There will always be more to do, especially with a large property. Like most people, we have limited time, skill sets, and budget. But good things usually take time. *Little by little.*

I think we pinched ourselves for the entire first year we lived here. Each season brought new surprises as we learned what was planted, what changed color, and what trees bore fruit. There wasn't a need to go to the park . . . our boys just opened the front, back, or side door. We roasted marshmallows around a campfire, and cousins and friends would come over to play capture the flag well past dark. We hid a puppy in the barn for our boys on Christmas morning and planted a vegetable garden in the spring.

Five years later, life continues to have its joys and challenges and ups and downs as it would anywhere. You can move past the city limits, but you can't move past the storms of life. How wonderful it is, though, to have a refuge from those storms, a sanctuary where family members can be together, exhale, and just be themselves.

I've often found it funny that the so-called *simple life* so many of us idealize actually requires quite a lot of work and time. Having acreage is a lot of upkeep. But as a friend who owns a five-acre farm nearby says, "It's a labor of love." (And if the flower garden beds are neglected, we reserve the right to call it a "country landscape.") As we learn to appreciate more about the seasons in nature, we're also learning more about the seasons in life. One can't do it all at the same time. Some seasons, life is challenging enough with just the day-to-day responsibilities. Home and yard projects get shelved for a while. Other times, we get on a roll (usually in spring after being cooped up all winter!), and our vision for the future takes hold again.

There is still a lot we would love to do to our home and acreage, but dreams are made in the space

of possibilities. And we're grateful for the space, which has enabled us to do things like make a baseball field, turn the hayloft into a home movie theater, plant a vegetable garden, and keep chickens and sheep. Even now, as I hear our sons laugh and play with one rowdy young dog and another beloved older dog out in the field, I whisper a prayer of thanks that we are blessed to call this place home.

> " If you haven't found it yet, keep looking. Don't settle. As with all matters of the heart, you'll know when you find it. "
>
> STEVE JOBS

Defining Your Dream Home and Acreage

LOCATION, LOCATION, LOCATION

Consider what is most important: privacy; landscape (open, treed, flat, water source, etc.); or proximity to town, work, and school.

◆

THE PROPERTY

Determine how much acreage is best-suited for your needs. Will you be gardening, farming, and/or keeping animals? What is manageable or desired?

◆

THE HOUSE

Decide on the size of house you are looking for. Is there a specific style (farmhouse, craftsman, historic, contemporary, etc.) you have in mind? Are you open to a fixer-upper, or does it need to be move-in ready?

◆

OUTBUILDINGS AND OTHER FEATURES

Keep in mind the "extras" that may be costly and time-consuming to later go back and add. Do you need a barn or workshop, fencing, a pool, or guest quarters?

CHAPTER 2

Farmhouse Style

"An empty room is a story waiting to happen, and you are the author."

CHARLOTTE MOSS

There's so much I love about farmhouse style. While relaxed and comfortable, it's also full of character and charm, often demonstrating an appreciation for the past. Mixing in vintage, one-of-a-kind pieces that have a story to tell adds personality—and often a soothing, aged patina—to a home. These thoughtful touches can take a house from purely functional to inspiring. And whether we're raising a family, working from home, or simply want a beautiful place to relax on the weekends, that inspiring space is the backdrop to so many of our dreams.

A farmhouse, where hearty meals were prepared and a good night's sleep assured, has long been the command center for the everyday workings of farm life. Today, there are many different ideas and interpretations of farmhouse style. Some people are drawn to an authentically timeworn, vintage farmhouse interior while others prefer the simpler, cleaner lines of a modern farmhouse design. Whichever style you lean toward, in its essence, farmhouse style is welcoming and designed for living. Some of the key places to focus your attention when capturing your personal farmhouse style include the front porch, furniture, textiles, walls, light fixtures, and accessories.

The Front Porch

Perhaps nothing epitomizes country living more than lemonade (or sweet tea if you live in the South) on the front porch. I picture a time when friends and neighbors dropped by (without calling or texting first) and visited all summer afternoon on wooden rockers. Our last home had only a small, covered entrance, so when we first viewed our farmhouse, we were very happy to discover it had a wraparound porch!

Since a porch is an extension of the house, and one of the first impressions of your home, it should be welcoming. Little touches like flowers or plants, a bench, and a wreath on the door will make for a happy entrance to invite people in. If your porch is covered, provide a feeling of warmth by layering doormats or rugs, and accessorizing with pillows and a throw blanket on a bench. Add a few seasonal touches and your porch will always look fresh and in harmony with nature.

A collection of galvanized buckets, tubs, and chicken water containers gives instant vintage charm to springtime herbs and flowers.

Furniture

Whether you're keeping cattle or raising a family, your furnishings will need to be workhorses themselves—unafraid of dirt and spills. While white furniture may seem counterintuitive to farm living, it is widely embraced these days. I enjoy white furniture like couches, chairs, and sectionals because they give my rooms an open and airy feel. I also prefer white furniture because instead of camouflaging dirt, it is easy to tell when cleaning is needed. (Just make sure your farmhouse whites come with slipcovers for easy washing!)

Slipcovers and Feed Sacks on Sofas, Sectionals, and Chairs

Though many wouldn't consider white furniture practical in a farmhouse setting, slipcovers that can easily be washed and bleached make it possible to live with white furniture without sacrificing your sanity. During the summer months, when our three sons are out of school and tend to bounce between the outdoors and indoors frequently, I wash our slipcovers about every three or four weeks. During the rest of the year, it may be every month or two as needed. In addition, I cover armrests with vintage feed or flour sacks. I enjoy the look of the added texture, and I especially like how they help keep the slipcovers clean longer!

Wood furniture embodies warmth and durability. While there are many wood finishes, I gravitate toward raw or weathered wood. One-of-a-kind dressers and hutches with chippy traces of paint provide interest and an acquired-over-time quality.

One of our favorite wood pieces in our home is an 1800s Swedish Mora clock we purchased for our tenth wedding anniversary. The hand-hewn wooden pieces and the natural wood color of the clock contribute toward a humble, but special, centuries-old heirloom piece we plan to keep in the family and enjoy for many years to come.

Whenever I purchase antique or vintage items, I ask where they came from because I want to learn more about their history. Another favorite wood piece in our home is an antique dresser that has been mostly stripped of its white paint. What does remain of the white paint adds to the character of the dresser. I was told that this dresser, which is often used in our entryway, was featured on the cover of *Southern Living* magazine many years ago. The lady I purchased it from (who prefers contemporary furnishings) had inherited it from her mother-in-law. Since it was only taking up space in her garage, she was willing to part with it for a good price.

Textiles

In farmhouse-style design, textiles are important. From linen duvet covers on beds to grain-sack table runners to lovingly created patchwork quilts on hand for picnics, textiles can be more than ordinary. They can be little luxuries that help make daily life feel special, because it is—each day is a gift.

" I am beginning to learn that it is the sweet, simple things of life which are the real ones after all."

LAURA INGALLS WILDER

There's something to be said about quality versus quantity when it comes to everyday items. I've begun collecting linen dishtowels and napkins, and have found a surprising second use for them. Not only are they long-lasting, natural choices for their intended purpose, but they also can be used as decor to soften the look of vignettes around the house. Display a folded stack of linen napkins on the shelf of a wood hutch. Drape a linen tea towel over a chair-back for an added layer of texture and lived-in charm. Even table linens can add a layer of warmth and comfort in a home.

Texture can change the whole feel of a room, making it cozy and inviting. I tend to use a lot of throw blankets in our living areas, especially in the cooler seasons. When not in use, the blankets are displayed

Blankets hung from an old orchard ladder are in easy reach, and pillows made from vintage work aprons add a sense of history to the room. A timeworn turkey crate serves as both a coffee table and a conversation piece.

on a vintage orchard ladder, again adding a layer of texture to the room. We also have folded blankets in baskets that are easily accessible. You can soften a wood chair or bench with a throw blanket. Hang a sweater from a coat rack, and use woven baskets for storage. Natural fiber and woven rugs provide comfort and warmth to wood floors, while upping the texture in a room.

Pillows are another easy way to add farmhouse style to your home. Grain-sack pillows have a subtle, nubby texture that makes you want to linger. You can repurpose vintage feed sacks, work aprons, and canvas bank bags into unique pillows. Ticking, floral, and checked fabrics can be mixed and matched to create a comfortable and welcoming space. Many of the pillows in our home have special meaning to me, since they were hand-sewn by my mother for special occasions, like wedding anniversaries and Christmas gifts. Pillows also provide a simple way to introduce a new color palette, making it easy to change the look of a room seasonally (or as often as you choose!).

Vintage European Grain Sacks

The soft oatmeal and straw colors and that great "nubby" texture of vintage grain sacks provide a European farmhouse feel that so many of us adore (shown on pages 22, 23, and 32). Part of the charm of grain sacks is from their history. Did you know that farmers used to deliver their product to be processed in these sacks, and then each bag was returned based on the striped pattern? Some grain sacks also have initials for identification. Grain sacks can be used to make table runners and pillows and add a touch of history to any room. You won't need to worry about their durability, since they were made to last and have already stood the test of time!

Walls

Let's not forget the walls! It's been said that the easiest way to change the look of a room is to paint it, and I agree. When we first moved into our farmhouse, the wall above the family room fireplace was a dark burgundy color. It demanded all the attention, and visually made your eyes stop. We painted the wall white, and then added white painted wood planks. The room instantly felt larger, brighter, and more cohesive.

On the other hand, you may love color and want a cozy or dramatic feeling in your home. Paint can help get you there. Just remember that paint colors will look different in each house, in each room, and even at different times of the day, depending on the amount of sunlight. When it comes to selecting a paint color, narrow down your possible paint colors to three or four, and purchase small samples of each. (It's worth the investment and much easier than having to go back and repaint an entire room, or living with a color you don't love.) Paint a swatch of each color on the wall and observe them at different times throughout the day. It may take several days to reach a decision, but better to be sure!

Using wood on walls gives character to a room. There are so many options for both materials and design. Shiplap and tongue-and-groove paneling are very similar, usually laid horizontally. The difference is in the way the boards connect. Board and batten is a design that has alternating wide boards with narrow strips. Board and batten also has a more formal, tailored look to it than shiplap and tongue and groove. Beadboard has narrower planks (usually installed vertically) connected similarly to tongue and groove but made in panels. Beadboard is casual in appearance and commonly found in cottages and farmhouses. There are also many styles of wainscoting or paneling that will add a layered dimension to walls.

When it comes to wall decor, there's no shortage of great choices. From mirrors to photographs and artwork to architectural elements, go with what you love. One common mistake that I saw a lot when I did home-staging work is hanging pictures that are too small for a space. Bigger is not always better, but when it comes to artwork, it usually is. If you have small pictures or paintings you want to hang, consider grouping them or creating a gallery-type wall. And remember, pictures should be hung at eye level. (I sometimes struggle with this, like many people. I want to hang pictures too high.) Because eye level depends on height, you can make it easier for yourself by assuming average eye level is about 5' 6".

My favorite decorating project in our home to date has been the gallery wall that goes up the stairway. I chose several favorite pictures of our sons and family and had them printed in black and white. Using simple black frames with white mattes keeps the focus on the people we love rather than on the colors. We can't help but look at those pictures every day and think back to special memories.

Shiplap

Tongue-and-groove

Board-and-batten

Beadboard

Our DIY natural wood shiplap wall and headboard made from vintage doors set the backdrop for a serene master bedroom. Ruffled bed linens and fresh white window treatments (sewn by my mom from drop cloths!) add layers of texture to this farmhouse bedroom.

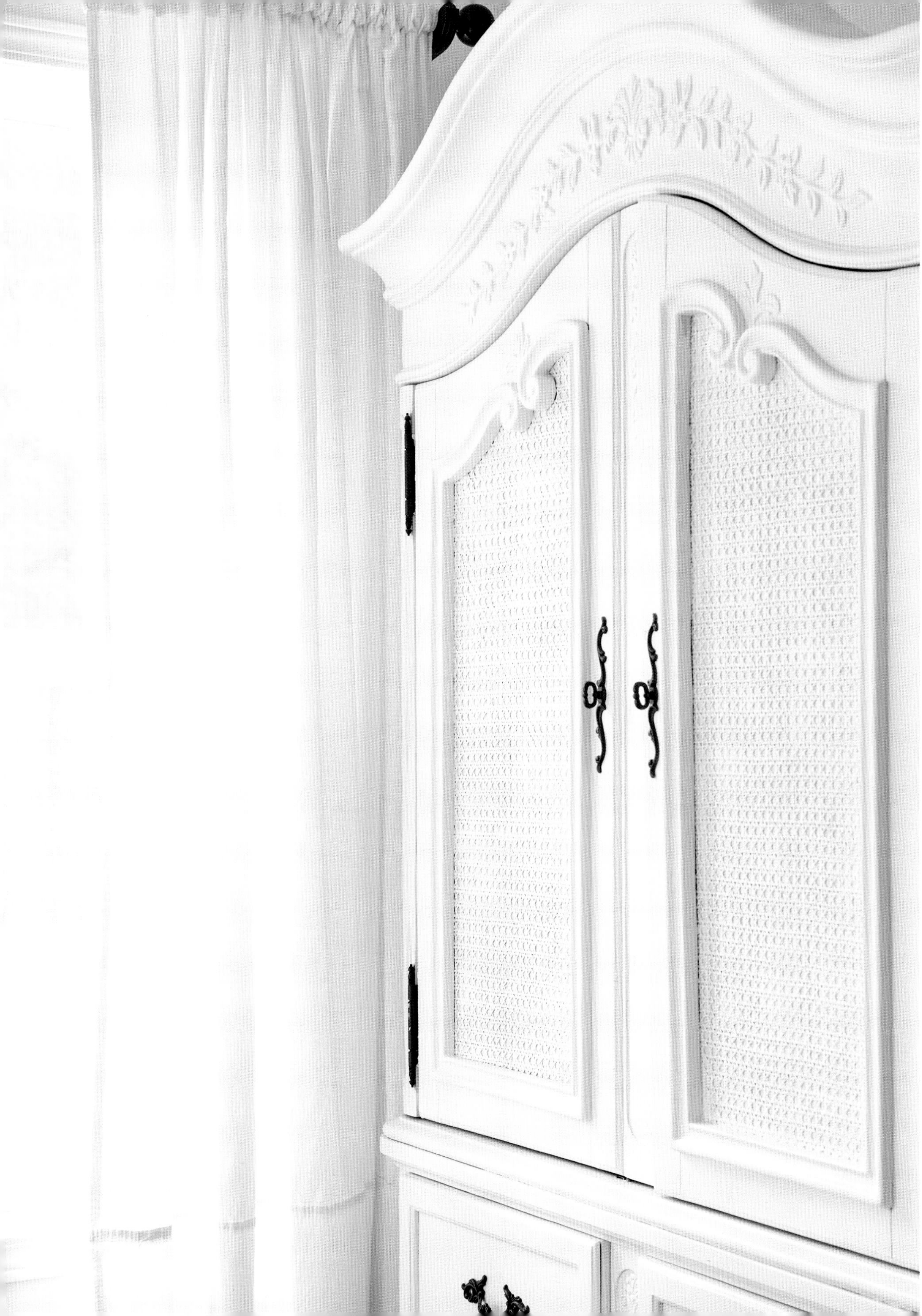

Light Fixtures

Lighting and light fixtures can really impact the feel of a room. After moving into our farmhouse, we replaced over a dozen dated, shell-shaped sconces throughout the house with vintage industrial sconces. The change was dramatic! For our stairway, I treated it as an accent wall, and chose black barn-light sconces to complement the black-and-white framed picture gallery wall. In our dining room, we chose a heavy wrought-iron antique chandelier for over the farm table. It was originally black, but I painted it white in keeping with the light and airy palette of the room. It took my husband, my sister, my brother-in-law and me to hang it (did I mention it was heavy?), but in the end, it was exactly the statement piece I'd envisioned.

Lighting styles include chandeliers, ceiling lights, lamps, and wall lights (or sconces). When considering lighting options, keep in mind scale and the role you want the fixture to play. How much light is needed?

Which style interests you (e.g., vintage-industrial, contemporary, traditional, farmhouse, etc.)? Are you looking for the star of the show (focal point of the space), or do you want something that will provide necessary light but blend into the room's environment? What about finishes? Are you open to having different finishes or are you trying to match the colors of other fixtures in the room or house? If you don't know where to start, flip through books and magazines until you find something you admire. Ask yourself the above questions to determine what it is you like about the fixture pictured and how it might work in your space.

If you're simply replacing light fixtures, that's easy enough to do on your own; just match the colored wires and follow the manufacturer's instructions. If you need to add lighting to a space where there is none, or you want to move the fixtures, then you'll need to call in the aid of an electrician.

Lighting also has a big impact on outbuildings, making outdoor areas more welcoming and usable when the sun goes down. We have a large gooseneck barn light mounted on the exterior of our gable-style barn. We had the light installed with day/night sensors. It feels like such a luxury, especially when I forget to close the sheep in the barn at night and have to go running out in the dark! Now the barn is well lit at night, and the light automatically turns off in the morning.

Painting a Light Fixture

Although spray paint can be used on most fixtures, I used a brush-on paint for our chandelier to provide heavier coverage because the wrought iron was so porous. Here are the simple steps:

1. Remove the light bulbs.

2. Clean the fixture with a damp cloth.

3. Paint at least two coats, allowing the paint to dry between coats. (I used three coats for ultimate coverage and alternated between a small bristle paintbrush, a sponge brush for dabbing, and a dry cloth for rubbing.)

4. After drying completely, replace the light bulbs and hang.

My go-to paint color for a clean-looking (non-creamy) white is Farrow and Ball All White or a similar pure white.

While beautiful light fixtures create both ambient lighting and decor statements, don't forget to add task lighting. Work spaces like your desk may require more direct light to make tasks easier. An articulating lamp can be positioned easily to shine light right where you need it.

Accessories and Styling

And now, the fun part of decorating—the finishing touches! (Though are you ever truly finished nesting?) Give a nod to the historic significance of farm life with accessories such as a basket of wooden eggs, farm tools, or vintage farm signs. Using weathered pieces in unexpected ways evokes a feeling of creativity and inspiration throughout a home. For example, a galvanized poultry waterer used for a pretty floral arrangement will add more personality and hints of life to a space than a standard glass vase. An antique chicken or turkey crate makes an interesting and practical coffee table. Hang a French market basket filled with fresh, dried, or faux flowers from a vintage farmhouse door. Incorporate a statement or conversational piece in each room, such as galvanized nesting boxes or a windmill, for a unique focal point. Show your love for a country landscape by bringing nature indoors—cherry blossom branches or peonies in spring, hydrangeas or lavender in summer, wheat bundles or leafy branches in the fall, and evergreen branches or pinecones in winter.

If you're a new home owner, have a limited budget (most of us do), or are in the process of changing your home's style, enjoy the hunt for furniture and accent pieces. Be careful when comparing your home to others. Remember that everyone is in a different situation. As they say, Rome wasn't built in a day, and neither will your ideal home be created overnight. In order to achieve an acquired-over-time, soulful interior, it actually does takes time.

A light and airy kitchen is brought to life with herbs and timeworn treasures, including a vintage French olive bucket and drying rack that holds Mason jar drinking glasses.

A cleaned section of sun-faded fencing is used as a
rustic headboard in our son Hudson's room. A wool rug
and army blanket add both warmth and rugged texture.

Kids' Rooms

Ideally, children's bedrooms should reflect their personality and interests. Our son Hudson has a collection of guitars, and Noah has a marquee letter *N* above his bedside table that helps personalize his room. A vintage-inspired "Ball Game Today" sign above the bed in our youngest son Lincoln's room is a simple nod to what he enjoys—playing ball! All three of our boys enjoy sports, so there are wall-mounted basketball hoops in two of their rooms, and the third son has sports canvases (wall art) and his trophies on display.

While our boys' bedrooms are not overtly farmhouse style, they do incorporate a few farmhouse design elements that help them blend in with the rest of our home. First, they each have wood furniture— some reclaimed, some natural, and some with a wood stain finish. Next, layered bedding provides an acquired-over-time feeling. And in keeping with the rest of the house, bedroom walls are kept light and airy (with the exception of one chalkboard wall).

Our tradition is that when our sons turn 12, they get a little room makeover, including a larger (full-size) bed. So far, two of our three boys have hit that milestone. I've found that it's a good idea with kids to narrow down options and let them make the final choice. For example, I might show them three bedding options (all of which I like, wink) and ask them which they like best. Everyone wins!

CHAPTER 3

Animal Menagerie

*" Animals are such agreeable friends—they ask
no questions; they pass no criticisms. "*

GEORGE ELIOT

I sometimes catch myself lingering to watch the chickens after I've given them their feed. Observing how they peck at their food—and each other (the pecking order is a legitimate thing!), and how they meander around their yard, completely in the moment, can be grounding and relaxing—especially on a busy or stressful day. The sheep baaing to greet us, the cats rubbing up against our legs for a pet, and the dogs dropping at our feet with their expectant eyes waiting for a belly rub all bring smiles to our faces. Animals add life and personality to our home. And there is something calming and comforting about farm animals.

From the time I was a little girl, I have had a soft spot for animals. Though I grew up on a cul-de-sac in California and not on a farm, I had chicks one spring, a lop-eared rabbit, hamsters, and our beloved and chubby family cat named Cushions. When I was 11 years old, my dream of owning a horse came true. I spent long afternoons at the barn where we boarded my Arabian–quarter horse mare, going on trail rides with friends and caring for my horse. Growing up I could be shy, but being around animals helped me relax. My animals always seemed happy to see me, and I could be myself with them.

When my own children started becoming interested in animals, we were living in a cul-de-sac on a fairly small lot. We gave them a bunny, which I think is a great animal for kids to start with. The rabbit lived outside in a raised wooden hutch. We brought him out often to play and run. Next, we added a kitten, and at the time, even that seemed like a big commitment with three sons, ages six and under. That same year, our oldest fell in love with his grandparents' chocolate Lab puppy, Buster. He begged us for a dog of his own. We visited Buster often. But it would be four more years until we found our

little farmstead and surprised our boys with their own Lab puppy on Christmas morning.

Having our boys grow up with animals has been a dream come true. People often ask me if our various animals serve a purpose (OK, mainly they're asking about the sheep!), or if it's just for the joy of having them. For us, it's a combination. It's been an interesting experience, seeing which animals can comingle and how each type of animal impacts our mini farm. Though we aren't experts, I'll share what we've discovered about the animals we keep, their needs, and their jobs here at our little farmstead.

Based on our experience, I have two general tips: First, unless you have very large amounts of time and resources to dedicate to your animals, introduce new types of animals one at a time. It will take a while to learn about the animals and how to best care for them. Keep in mind that time and care requirements may change with the season. Second, animals typically do better with two or more of their type. After all, animals like sheep and chickens are both flock animals. Having more than one not only provides companionship but also offers safety from predators.

Dogs

Buster (remember the chocolate Lab puppy our son fell in love with?) now lives with us, alongside our younger yellow Lab, Ford. They have brought so much joy to our sons—and to our whole family. As far as filling a practical need, they are effective guard dogs. They let us know if any person or animal ventures onto our property. Their needs include what you would expect for dogs: food, water, shelter, exercise, attention, basic grooming, and regular veterinarian care.

Cats

We typically have between two to four barn cats at any given time. They're mixed-breed, domestic cats that live in our barn and on the surrounding property. While somewhat friendly, barn cats aren't as attached to humans as house cats would be. Their job is to control the rodent and mole population in the barn, and they are professionals! We provide them with food, water, and veterinarian care, as needed.

Chickens

There are few things that make a property feel more like a country setting than having chickens roaming around. They are entertaining to watch, and can even be friendly. We purchased our chicks from local feed shops the first spring we lived at our little farmstead. It was so exciting for our boys, then ages four, eight, and ten. We kept our chicks under a heat lamp in a stock tank, with bedding, in our laundry room for the first few weeks. Their happy chirping cheered up

The ducks and a chicken enjoy free-range time near the coop (left). Noah holding the family Easter bunny (above left). Our yellow Lab, Ford, as a puppy (above right).

Animal Menagerie | 45

many gray, early spring days here in the Seattle area. As the chicks grew bigger, we moved them to the tack room inside the barn (still in the stock tank). Once the chicks were fully feathered (about seven to eight weeks old), they were ready to move to the chicken coop, where they could spend their days outside and their nights inside the coop.

For more on the specifics of keeping chickens, see "Caring for Chickens" below and "Chicken Breeds" on page 47.

CARING FOR CHICKENS

To care for chickens, you will need a predator-proof coop for shelter. Inside the coop should be nesting boxes (a quiet, dark place where the hens go to lay their eggs), roosting bars (where the chickens perch

for the night), a place for food (chicken feeder) and the feed itself, and a chicken waterer with clean water. You will also need some type of a chicken run if your chickens are not going to be free range. The run should be a protected area where the chickens can get exercise, sunshine, and fresh air. The run should have at least a patch of dry ground for the chickens to take dust baths, which helps prevent parasites.

If you are beginning with chicks, you will need a draft-free brooder box—a place to keep chicks safe, warm, and away from any older chickens or predators. We've used different things over the years, from a cardboard box to a galvanized stock tank. Feed shops also sell specialty brooders. You'll need chick bedding (like pine shavings), a heat lamp, a waterer, a feeder, and chick starter for the chicks to eat.

Chicken Breeds

Over the years, we've had several different breeds of chickens. With a little experience under my belt, I now select certain breeds based on the eggs they produce, their appearance, and how well they have done at our little farmstead.

LAVENDER ORPINGTON chickens (top) have a beautiful pale grayish-lavender color. They are large in size with a fluffy appearance (lots of feathers!). Lavender Orpington chickens have a friendly temperament and good egg production (up to 200 a year according to the Happy Chicken Coop website).

RHODE ISLAND REDS (second from top) are a healthy breed who are also good egg layers. They can be friendly, and sometimes a little pushy. We have one Rhode Island Red who will often run to meet us, as if she's been waiting for our visit.

BARRED PLYMOUTH ROCK CHICKENS (third from top) are stunning with their black and white stripes. They are also good egg layers (notice a trend here with our favorite breeds?) with a pleasant disposition.

DELAWARE chickens (fourth from top) are white with black edging on some of their feathers. They have bright red combs and wattles. You may have guessed it, but they are good egg layers too. Charlotte, one of our Delaware chickens who was part of our original little flock, once went missing. I thought a predator had gotten to her and was feeling sad, especially since she was one of our original chickens. That evening, my husband said, "Ah, Julie . . . I think someone is at the door for you." To my surprise, Charlotte, who had never been to the front of our property, had found her way up our steps, onto the porch, and was waiting right in front of the front door, like a little lady. It looked as if she had just rung the doorbell. I was so happy to see her!

AMERAUCANA chickens (fifth from top) lay eggs in shades of blue and green. This makes gathering and gifting eggs a lot more fun (in my opinion). From an aesthetic point of view, our Ameraucanas have not been real lookers, but their eggs make up for it.

We have had **SILKIE** chickens (bottom) before, and I love the way they look. They have a really fluffy plumage and are soft (like silk!) to the touch. They look like they are wearing slippers and having a fabulous high-volume hair day. Silkies are smaller in size and lay small eggs. We haven't had Silkie chickens for the last few years, because due to their size, they are usually the first to be picked off by predators.

FRESH EGGS

There's just something about farm-fresh eggs. My husband wasn't overly excited about us keeping chickens—that is, until he first tasted those fresh eggs! They are full of flavor and protein, and it's hard to go back to store-bought, pale-yellow–yoked eggs after having the real deal. (We're a little partial.)

Speaking of fresh eggs, how can you tell how fresh an egg really is? Crack an egg open, into a pan or a bowl. A fresh egg yolk will stand up, while an older egg yolk will flatten. Perhaps you've gathered dozens of eggs, and as you reach into the fridge to get a few for your recipe, you start to wonder which eggs are freshest or if any have gone bad. There's a simple test you can do. Fill a large bowl with water, and

carefully place your eggs (uncooked) in the water. The freshest eggs will lie on the bottom. Eggs that are a few weeks old may appear to be "standing" on the bottom vertically. Very old eggs will float to the top, because older eggs have bigger air cells.

How long will your farm-fresh eggs last? It may be helpful to understand how old supermarket eggs can be. The United States Department of Agriculture dictates that an egg can be sold for up to 30 days after it was packed in a carton. Farmers have 30 days from the time the egg is laid to put it in the carton. This means that by the time you buy them, store-bought eggs can be up to two months old. Unless they smell bad, the eggs are fine to eat, just not nearly as fresh as those you gather from your coop!

In addition to enjoying farm-fresh eggs ourselves, we find that they make wonderful gifts. Rather than reusing grocery-store cartons with another farm's labeling, I order biodegradable cartons with room for a half dozen eggs. You can customize a stamp that tells about your chickens, coop, farm, or eggs. Tie with baker's twine and add a flower or herb sprig for a beautiful and practical little farm-fresh gift.

Our chickens usually start laying eggs at about five to six months old. Many chickens lay an egg every day or two, up until they are three or four years old, when egg laying decreases or stops altogether. Hens (female chickens) do not need a rooster (male chicken) to lay eggs. And if there is a rooster living with the hens, it does not impact their egg-laying schedule. (However, if there is a rooster living with the hens, there is a possibility that the eggs may be fertilized. While some people may get a little squeamish thinking about this, it is perfectly fine to consume fertilized eggs. If you gather your eggs every day and keep them in the fridge, they will no longer change or develop.)

ROOSTERS

While our intention was to raise only hens, it's often difficult, even for trained professionals, to determine a baby chick's gender at just a few days old. Thus, we have had a rooster or two in our flock at times.

Roosters generally aren't permitted inside city limits due to their early morning wake-up calls, but we live just past the city limits, so we decided to keep them. The benefits of having a rooster or two is that they're protective of the hens and will defend them against predators. We actually enjoy their crowing, as we feel it adds to a rural atmosphere. Interestingly, the roosters also act as a sort of watchdog, making noises when something or someone approaches unexpectedly or if the roosters perceive danger.

The potential downside to having a rooster is that you need to stay on top of gathering eggs in case they have been fertilized (unless you are trying to produce chicks instead of eggs, of course). The other negative to keeping a rooster is that they can be aggressive with hens or people, depending on their personality.

Developing your ideal flock will take some time and experimentation. Questions worth considering are: How many chickens and eggs are ideal for my lifestyle and property, and which breeds do I most enjoy based on their beauty, temperament, and egg production?

Ducks

One of our sons had been asking for a pet duck for a few years. While we were picking up a batch of chicks from our local feed shop, we spotted the most adorable Pekin ducklings, and I gave in. Let me just tell you that they were so cute and fun to have that first spring! We kept them with our chicks and would let them out to play a couple of times a day, and they'd literally follow our boys around the house.

When the ducks were grown, we moved them out to the chicken yard with the chickens. They did well together for about nine months, but as the ducks got older, they became aggressive with the chickens. We simply partitioned off part of the chicken run to make a separate area for them. Part of this behavior could

be because both of our ducks are male, even though we thought we were buying females. So not only do our ducks need their own space, but they're not producing eggs.

If you are raising ducks for egg production, here are some fun facts. Did you know that duck eggs are larger than chicken eggs and higher in protein? Their shells are also tougher than chicken eggs, so they have a longer shelf life.

Since our two male ducks are not producing eggs, their purpose is purely as pets. Ducks require a predator-proof area, feed (ours eat the same layer crumble as our chickens), and water. They also need water to swim in (we use a large stock tank) and some shelter.

Sheep

I don't know how I first became interested in (OK fine, *fell in love with*) Olde English "Babydoll" Southdown sheep, but I think it was simply from seeing pictures of them. It's hard not to fall for their petite stature (full grown they are just 18 to 24 inches at the shoulders), fluffy wool, teddy bear appearance, and "perma-smiles." And if it's a pastoral setting you're after, what could be better than sheep?

The first four springs we lived in our farmhouse, I contacted Babydoll Southdown sheep breeders to ask for information, hoping to add some to our little farm. But it wasn't until our fifth spring at our little farmstead that we visited the most beautiful ranch in Northern California and were able to spend some time with Babydoll Southdown lambs. As you can imagine, this made our boys really want them too!

A few weeks after returning from that trip, we purchased three lambs from that California ranch.

Because Babydoll Southdown sheep are small, they don't require a huge area of land. Our sheep live in one of our barn stalls and have access to three outdoor paddock areas (about 30 by 80 feet) outside the barn during the day. We also let them out to graze on our property's pasture, but have to monitor them since only the paddocks currently have sheep fencing. It's important to know that sheep are near the bottom of the food chain, which makes them a fairly easy target for predators. We have to be aware of not only the coyotes and bobcats that sometimes roam through our property, but also any dogs. Even the sweetest family dog's instincts can take over and cause it to attack a sheep. We choose to close our sheep in the barn each night for their protection.

If you're wondering what the purpose of keeping sheep is, first of all they are beloved pets with sweet temperaments. Each of our sheep has his own distinct personality. Our sons are learning to help care for them, which we believe is a good life lesson. The sheep also help us trim grass in some areas of our property. In addition, we are learning about ways to use their wool.

If you are considering sheep, they will need shelter (we use our barn, but a three-sided structure is sufficient), bedding (we use straw), pasture, predator-proof fencing, feed (we use second-cut orchard grass, which is soft and high in protein), fresh water, and salt.

Keeping sheep healthy also includes trimming their hooves periodically to prevent foot rot, deworming as needed, and shearing once a year. It is necessary to check on sheep at least twice a day, observing their overall health and keeping your eye out for signs of bloat (gas accumulation that can be lethal), lethargy, or any unusual behavior.

I recommend consulting with your veterinarian to determine what your sheep need based on where you live. The first week we had our lambs, we had a vet come to our property to immunize them, evaluate their health, and inspect our pasture for any vegetation that could be harmful to sheep. Having a relationship with a vet you can rely on can really put your mind at ease. To keep costs down, call the vet right away if you suspect that one of your sheep is ill. Don't wait until evening. After-hours emergency visits are expensive!

Also, try to combine care when possible. For example, if you pay for a shearer (rather than shearing yourself), ask him or her to also trim the sheeps' hooves. We've been told Babydoll sheep hoof trimming is not difficult once you get the hang of it, but we have yet to learn. At this point, we're content to pay for the service.

So far, having sheep has been a wonderful experience for us. When our chicks were too little to move to the big coop but too big to be kept indoors, we moved them out of our house and in with the sheep, and they all got along just fine. And one of our barn cats, Rosemary, enjoys being near the sheep. We joke that she babysits them and feels responsible for them. (We're happy for the help!)

Although our property is set up for horses, at this point in our lives—raising three children who are all involved in multiple activities—we just don't have the time. (My 11-year-old self would never understand!)

Part of the beauty of having acreage is that in many ways, you can create your own environment. While animals require daily time and care (not always enjoyable during Seattle's long rainy season), the animals—with their unique personalities, needs, and contributions—help us form another layer of connection with our home and land. They are one more thing that our family of five shares together. The laughter and stories about the animals' antics, assisting each other with chores, and learning about the animals as a family all help us grow deeper roots right here, where we are planted.

Knitted Hats

Ever since getting our Babydoll sheep, I dreamed of having their wool turned into yarn and having hats knitted for our three boys. (I had no idea about the process of turning wool into yarn, but figured there had to be a way!) I was blessed to find someone who was up for the challenge. We had only very short lambswool from our first shear. (Many mills require a minimum length of 3"—ours was nowhere near that long!) As if that weren't enough, it was November and I hoping to have finished hats by Christmas. (Most mills require 6 to 12 months for processing!)

I quickly learned the main steps from sheep to yarn are sheering, skirting the fleece to remove all unwanted bits and pieces, washing the wool, carding the wool to open up the locks, creating a roving (a narrow bundle of fiber for spinning), and finally spinning the roving into yarn.

I was so excited to receive the skeins of yarn! Each was marked with, "Teddy," "Winston," or "George," the names of our sheep. I passed off the yarn to two talented ladies, who quickly knit three hats in time for Christmas Eve. What precious keepsakes!

CHAPTER 4

Country Landscape and Garden

" I long for the countryside. That's where I get my calm and tranquility—from being able to come and find a spot of green. "

EMILIA CLARKE

To me, "the country" conjures up images of lilacs, orchards, vineyards, golden wheat fields whispering in the late summer breeze, old apple trees with twisting branches, and sun-faded farmhouses with their lived-in charm. I picture expansive pastures where farm animals graze and golden sunflowers reach up to the sky. And there's nothing that puts my mind at ease like a drive down a barn-dotted country road, where clothes dry outside on a line, and time seems to stand still. Warm, early fall days bring colorful pumpkins and row after row of dried cornstalks, preparing us for the first frost, and a harvest moon that brings bright light to the night sky. What is it that fills us with nostalgia about this countryside scenery?

Perhaps now more than ever, we recognize the disparate cultures of modern city life versus the simple country life of days gone by. As technology races forward, affording us the ability to be continuously "connected," isn't it natural that we might crave connecting with what is presently in front of us? Don't we yearn for time to notice the beauty of nature, breathe in the fresh air, and be alone with our thoughts and dreams? Instead of connecting digitally and remotely, to actually take a walk, or enjoy a meal outdoors with family and friends? This is the country backdrop we envisioned, and found, just past the city limits.

*The natural beauty of the land often stops us in our tracks, from the maple trees' show
of golden changing leaves to the bountiful produce found in the garden and on fruit trees.*

When our realtor, along with the home seller (who was acting as her own realtor) first showed us this property, my husband and I were in awe of the beautiful acreage. (Now might be a good time for me to confess that I can hardly recount this memory without my face flushing red with embarrassment.) There were large areas of grass, many, many flower beds, pretty trees, a stone wall border near the gravel driveway, arbors and trellises dripping with lush vines, and a well-kept riding arena. It was a picture-perfect, 2.3 acre setup. And then I asked the question only a naive-but-hopeful suburban thirty-something would: "So, is the upkeep here pretty manageable, or how much time would you say it takes to keep up the yard?" I saw the seller shoot our agent a look. Even then, I knew by the way she searched for the right words to answer, that we had no idea of the work it would take to maintain this property to the degree that we were seeing it. And we didn't.

What I've come to realize is that when acreage is maintained beautifully, it may appear (at least to the novice) that the property is being seen in its natural state. When weeds aren't visible in the flower beds, you may not think about how many hours went into that achievement. And when the trees have all been pruned to their correct size, you may be tempted to think that's just how they grow. You might also surmise that the grass doesn't grow quickly. And surely the beautiful sand in the riding arena wouldn't be covered in vegetation five short years from now when a trampoline for the kids would replace the beautiful Arabian horses—right?

Yes, actually, it would. And it is. But it's OK; it's still beautiful, just in a less manicured sort of way. We are enjoying our property, and we recognize that there are various seasons in life. Since our days are very full right now raising our three sons, we do what we can but try to embrace a more natural, country landscape full of grace and lived-in charm rather than a meticulously maintained formal garden. During the warmer months, my husband practically lives on the riding mower, which, thankfully, he finds relaxing. And I've enjoyed learning more about which flowers and vegetables grow best here. We look forward to doing more with the property over time and are thankful that the land isn't going anywhere.

Growing Vegetables

For the first few years, our young children happily helped me plant the vegetable garden and each child had his own raised garden bed. We'd watch with excitement as seeds and starts grew into plants that produced a variety of vegetables. These days, I am the one who most enjoys tending the vegetable garden, though we have a tradition of planting it as a family on Mother's Day each spring. (Notice how I work in that gift of quality time together as a tradition? It's harder for people to wiggle out of it that way! Just a tip.)

Living in the Pacific Northwest, we're in USDA plant hardiness zone 8. (The plant hardiness zonal map was created to give gardeners an indication of how hardy the plants you grow will be.) You may be surprised to know that Texas, which has a very different climate than ours in the Seattle area, is also in hardiness zone 8! I've recently learned that the zone refers to the average winter minimum temperature. So while people who live in zone 8 may have success with similar plants, their growing seasons will be unique to where they live geographically. For example, not much grows from November to February where we live, whereas in much of Texas, the intense heat of late summer makes July and August their off-season for gardening. For our family in the Pacific Northwest, making sure the vegetable garden is planted by Mother's Day at the very latest (preferably by April) has been a good rule of thumb.

Admittedly, we didn't know much about gardening before moving to a property with space for growing,

and it's a joy to continue to learn more each year. I'll never forget that first year's harvest! You could not wipe the proud smiles off our boys' faces as they held their produce up triumphantly. And greens they would never eat from the store—well, they were willing to try them from their garden.

SEEDS VS. STARTS

When planting our vegetable garden, we use a combination of seeds and starts. (Starts are simply plants that have already begun to grow—or started—in a greenhouse setting.) Since seeds are more affordable, and seed packets usually yield many plants, they're a good option for vegetables that are easy to grow from seed and that you want in abundance. Vegetables that are easy to grow from seeds include lettuce, zucchini, cucumbers, peas, and beans. Plants that take longer to mature are best grown from starts—especially if you live in a region where the growing season is short—or started in a greenhouse, if you have one, where you can raise plants from seeds in a protected environment and controlled climate.

Planting in Tubs

Raised beds of any sort help keep the soil warmer, which is important for a northern climate. This past year, I planted our lettuce in a large oval galvanized stock tank. The lettuce did very well and was better protected from the many rabbits that call our property home.

During mid-to-late summer, we are greatly rewarded for time invested in the vegetable garden. It's the time of year I wish we could freeze the garden! (See pages 58 and 59).

"There are no gardening mistakes, only experiments."

Janet Kilburn-Phillips

For plants that do take longer to mature, we buy starts from a local nursery. We have used starts for tomato plants, corn, peppers, and sometimes even lettuce. Starts are a great option for when you only want a few of one type of vegetable plant and don't need a whole packet of seeds. Since starts are more mature than seeds, their rate of success is higher. If you've planted seeds in the past without much success, try growing those veggies in your garden again, but next time, buy starts. Starts are easier to care for because they are visible above the soil.

If you need another reason to begin with starts, they make it easy to fill in your garden when you are expecting visitors or want to take photographs! They can also be a visual encouragement during those first several weeks in the spring when you're waiting for seedlings to germinate and grow. It's nice to actually see something other than dirt in the garden! You may want to experiment with planting both seeds and starts of the same variety to see how well they do in your garden. Doing so will also give you multiple harvest dates.

PREPPING THE GARDEN

It can be easy to underestimate the time it will take to prepare the ground, plant the garden, and then maintain it by watering and weeding throughout the growing season. Someday, I dream of having a full-on pumpkin patch (not to mention a little Christmas tree field!), but for now, we grow a few pumpkins in our raised garden beds, and we trek to the mountains to cut down our Christmas tree.

If you don't have a readymade bed, you may have to dig one, removing sod and amending the soil to make it a great spot for growing plants of all sorts. That's where raised beds come in. You don't have to remove the sod—you can build sides and add topsoil right over the grass, which will die off under the darkness and weight of the soil.

I've heard it said that gardening is a mix of science and art. I agree! It requires planning, observation, experimentation, and care. Our vegetable garden looks a little different each year. This past year, we planted hundreds and hundreds of wildflower seeds on the perimeter of the vegetable garden. It felt like a mini Christmas—our surprise gifts were flowers popping up throughout late summer and into early fall.

A Beginner's Vegetable Garden

When beginning a vegetable garden, it helps to start with a small area, choose your favorite vegetables, and see how they do. Perhaps you want to start with a salad garden and grow lettuce, tomatoes, cucumbers, and carrots? Do you enjoy baking with zucchini? One of the easiest vegetables to grow, zucchini is great for beginning gardeners. Do your children or grandchildren like to snack on sugar snap peas? Grow them and invite kids to harvest (pick) their own to eat! They're delicious right out of the garden, warm from the sun.

The vegetables we've had the most success with are zucchini, tomatoes, cucumbers, lettuce, sugar snap peas, snow peas, carrots, and pumpkins. Herbs like rosemary, lavender, mint, cilantro, and thyme have also grown well in our garden.

7 EASY-TO-GROW VEGETABLES AND HOW WE PLANT THEM

Zucchini. Seeds because they are easy to grow.

Tomatoes. Starts because we usually need only two or three tomato plants.

Cucumbers. Seeds, again, because they are easy to grow.

Lettuce. Seeds and starts because both grow well and will provide you with different harvest dates, extending your salad season. (Plus, starts make your new garden look a little bit more established.)

Peas (sugar snap or snow peas). Seeds or starts both work well. If they're on sale, might as well get the starts for a head "start" on your garden.

Green beans. Seeds or starts, same as above.

Carrots. Seeds because root vegetables do not transplant well.

Colorful peppers
grow on a simple
trellis we constructed
from fallen branches
on our property.

Bumper crops of grapes and apples are some of the simple country joys we pictured when moving here.

Growing Fruit

Since we moved into our home during the fall, it was exciting to see all the different varieties of plants, trees, and flowers we had on our property that first spring and summer. We were delighted to find cherry, apple, pear, and peach trees. And along the backyard trellis, grapes and hops grow in abundance. While the grapes are mostly ornamental, we enjoy snacking on them and feeding them to the chickens, who go crazy for them! (That's one of the little joys of farm life—watching the food chain in real time. We grow the grapes and feed them to the chickens. The chickens eat the grapes and lay the eggs. We eat the eggs . . . and on it goes!)

Fruit trees need some tending to get the best results. It may seem counterproductive to prune your tree or cull some of the early starts when you're excited to harvest those cherries and plums later in the season. However, giving space for the fruit to grow will yield bigger and heartier fruits rather than lots of little ones. Pruning fruit trees depends on what types of trees you have, so I recommend asking at your local nursery or reading up on pruning at the library.

The Flower Garden

We were blessed to move to a place with so many established beautiful plantings. There are certain flowers that just seem to embody country living. And as you'll see, many of them feature lavender or purple blooms.

"To plant a garden is to believe in tomorrow."

AUDREY HEPBURN

LILACS

You can catch me regularly stalking our lilac bushes in spring, keeping careful tabs on when these fragrant beauties will be in bloom. Lilac varieties range from white to pale pink to lavender and deep purple. We have a few different varieties and their scent is, quite simply, spring.

If lilacs grow quickly in your climate as they do in ours, be sure to prune them after they bloom in the spring. Otherwise, they can grow quite tall and the blooms will be out of reach! You won't want to miss out on the fragrance—or the chance to cut some fresh lilacs to enjoy indoors. Just don't wait until fall to prune, or you may not have blooms the next spring.

WISTERIA

Wisteria is another of my favorite flowering plants. It's a woody vine with blossoms that hang dramatically from arbors, and it has a romantic, old-fashioned quality about it. We have both purple and white wisteria on our property.

I'm surprised by the number of comments I receive about wisteria and how quickly it can take over. While it is true that wisteria vines grow quickly and can work their way into crevices and onto the roof, let me assuage any fears—if you trim it back, it won't take over. You won't go to sleep one night with a neat little wisteria shrub and wake up the next morning with a vine-covered roof; you will have warning and time to prune. That being said, a mature wisteria plant's twisting branches can become very heavy, so it requires a solid structure to grow against. I love the look of wisteria, and to me, the natural aesthetic is worth the maintenance.

Wisteria grows best in full sun. We have purple wisteria growing on a wooden arbor in the back of our house, where it receives partial morning sun and full afternoon sun. It's happy and so am I because I can see it from the kitchen window as well as when I'm outdoors.

Toward the front of our property, near the vegetable garden, we have white wisteria, which receives full sun throughout the day. For information on how to manage wisteria, see "Caring for Wisteria" on page 70.

LAVENDER

As a self-professed Francophile, lavender makes me very happy. This flowering perennial (it grows back every year) has a beautiful, soothing scent and looks pretty either fresh or dried. While it's not classified as an herb due to its woody stem, it can be used as

Caring for Wisteria

I'm not a trained gardener or horticulture expert, but after living with a mature wisteria for several years, here's what we've learned about keeping it pruned and tidy.

Prune in winter when the leaves and flowers are gone so you can see the vine and how it's growing. If you inherit an older wisteria, you can prune it way back to get it under control—but don't do it all at once. Pruning a bit each year for a couple of years puts less stress on the vine.

In summer, when the vine is actively growing, you may need to prune to keep it in bounds. Prune off any unruly parts of the vine that are growing in a direction you don't want them to head. And prune to thin things out a bit. It may seem counterproductive to having lots of flowers, but if you prune away some buds, the plant can spend more energy making the remaining flowers grow bigger. Plus, they'll have more access to sunlight, which is needed for blooming to occur.

You don't need to prune every week, but when stray vines impact the look you want, reach for your clippers. Unless you cut the plant back to less than three feet tall, you really can't ruin it!

an herb and looks right at home in an herb garden, as well as in several other locations around the yard.

Just as with lilacs and wisteria, the colors of lavender varieties vary from white to palest lavender to dark purple. We grow English and French lavender, which are both quite hardy. We also enjoy planting Spanish lavender in containers. Once lavender is established (after a year), it doesn't require much care or watering aside from available rainfall, unless you grow it in containers. Then the soil can dry out more quickly, so plan to water it as you would with any container gardens.

Depending on your climate, lavender may grow exceedingly well (it's a member of the mint family, which is quite well known for growing and spreading!), so don't be afraid to trim it back. Cut the stems and enjoy the color and fragrance indoors, or dry them to use in sachets. Prune lavender in summer after it flowers. You can cut back about half the height, but don't cut into the woody stems.

Where to Plant Lavender

+ Plant lavender in containers on the porch so that visitors are greeted with a pleasant scent at the door.

+ Planting fragrant perennials, such as lavender and rosemary, in close proximity to the animal areas will help mitigate some of the unpleasant scents that animals produce. (Just keep in mind that if the animals can access the plants, they may think you've provided them a special snack!)

+ Include lavender with or without other herbs in your vegetable garden. It's attractive to pollinators, so that's a good thing!

HYDRANGEAS

Looking for another romantic choice for a farmhouse setting? Choose hydrangeas. Their blooms are relatively long-lasting and can be dried for enjoyment year-round. Hydrangea varieties offer a bunch of different colors, from white to blue to pink, and even chartreuse, and blossom shapes come in mop head and conical varieties. Depending on your soil type, the colors will be more or less intense or even change from what you saw at the nursery. I love the romance and old-fashioned charm of white hydrangeas and have a row of them growing along the front porch railing.

BULBS

Don't forget to plant bulbs each fall that will become the first signs of spring on your farmstead! Be generous with daffodils, hyacinths, tulips, crocuses, and allium. They'll be your reward by blooming year after year when planted in beds with good drainage. My mom has a sweet tradition of planting bulbs with

The Easiest Way to Dry Hydrangeas

When drying hydrangeas, it's (almost) all about when you cut the flowers. Make sure you don't cut them too soon. For best drying results, hydrangeas should have already started to dry on the shrub. They are ready when some of the petals have turned delicate and papery.

Once cut, NEVER put them in water. I used to think that I could dry hydrangeas that I had already enjoyed for several days in a vase with water. I ended up with wilted, disheveled blooms. Instead, once you've cut your hydrangeas, simply place them in an empty (dry) vase, jar, or container. They will dry beautifully. Remember that blooms will fade if they are in direct sunlight. I happen to like the sun-faded look, but retaining more color requires moving them away from windows.

our kids when my husband and I go away for the night, once a year, to celebrate our anniversary. It's the gift that keeps on giving, and I think of my mom when I see the colorful blooms in spring.

SUNFLOWERS

Few flowers are as fun to watch grow as sunflowers. We watch with wonder as they grow far above our heads. Their bright, golden-yellow color and large "faces" seem to be smiling at us through the windows as summer fades to fall. I think sunflowers may be the happiest flowers of all. And when fall rolls around, if you don't harvest the seeds, the birds will enjoy them too.

ROSES, PEONIES, AND MORE

We have a few roses and peonies, which are beautiful, fragrant choices for classic, country-style gardens. If you want to add roses to your garden, look for shrub roses or a climbing rose for old-fashioned charm.

We also enjoy our little wildflower/cutting garden bed, which included annuals like zinnias, poppies, and bachelor's buttons, to name a few. I hope to increase the variety of wildflowers next year. And speaking of hopes and dreams for the garden, I love the weeks between late winter and early spring, when it's time to start planning the coming year's garden . . . .

CHAPTER 5

Seasonal Living

"When the seasons shift, even the subtle beginning, the scent of a promised change, I feel something stir inside me. Hopefulness? Gratitude? Openness? Whatever it is, it's welcome."

KRISTIN ARMSTRONG

Seasonal living takes on a whole new meaning when you live on acreage. We have become more aware and appreciative of seasonal beauty since moving to our little farmstead. We are also more mindful of chores that need to get done while nature is on our side! We love watching the changing outdoor scenery, and enjoy celebrating the seasons with some special traditions, which include bringing seasonal touches indoors. Learning how to more fully embrace the seasons gives our lives a more natural rhythm

In spring, the whole world seems to be coming to life! Rabbits run and hop all through the bright green spring grass and beneath the new foliage. Chirping birds fill the air with their songs during the day. As the sun begins to fade, the birds' melodies give way to the frogs, who provide the evening soundtrack of spring. We plant our vegetable garden and enjoy new blooms as spring turns into summer. Eating outdoors with family and friends is one of the highlights of summer. Long, warm days produce a harvest of vegetables and fruit. We enjoy s'mores by a campfire.

Then in fall, as leaves turn golden, we pick pumpkins for the porch, and move sweaters to the front of our closets. As the weather turns cooler, it's cozy indoors with candles, blankets, and a fire in the fireplace. Winter brings the excitement of Christmas and then a calming stretch of "hunkering down." The garden is dormant, and most of our time is spent indoors. We savor a few days of snow here in the Pacific Northwest, and then turn hopeful for the promise of spring.

Crocuses are among the first spring blooms in the garden (above left).
Our Babydoll Southdown lambs enjoy their first spring (above center).
Our boys set up a baseball field in the pasture with their dad (above right).

Spring

Just when we think winter did in the garden once and for all, the hellebores and crocus surprise us with their early spring blooms. There's nothing like that first sighting of new life. After a long winter, it feels like this event should make the local news. Nature is waking up!

FLOWERS AND FROGS AND MUD, OH MY!

Soon the daffodils rise from the damp earth with an explosion of yellow. Cherry blossoms, in shades of pink and white, are a visual delight against a bright blue spring sky. Birds sing as the days get longer, and there's more time to spend outside after school and work before it gets dark. But one thing in particular that happens each year will forever remind me of spring in the country: As it starts getting warmer and I open the windows to let in some fresh evening air, I'm greeted by a chorus of frogs who seem to be announcing the arrival of spring. I call to our boys to come listen, and I wonder if they're also imagining a scene from a Beatrix Potter book.

In the Northwest, our winter days are very short. So spring brings with it the feeling that we now have a massive addition to our house, which is the two+ acre yard. Doors fly open, and out run three boys to kick around a soccer ball, shoot hoops, or ride bikes. Spring is the time of year we've been known to make a baseball field in the side pasture, and dream up plans for the garden amidst muddy boots and even muddier dogs. Most springs we add a few chicks to our flock, and one spring even included our new lambs.

SPRINGTIME INDOORS

In the farmhouse, spring includes cut lilacs in vintage containers, and greenery of all sorts. Bring on the flowers and plants—life is in full bloom! Add in some handcrafted, intricately designed wooden eggs my dad brought us from Europe, and a lovingly painted wooden cross that one of our boys made for Easter. Soon Mimi (as our kids call my mom) will be dropping off her delicious homemade orange-coconut Easter coffee cake, still warm from the oven.

Mimi's Orange-Coconut Easter Coffee Cake

SERVES 10–12

CAKE	DIRECTIONS
1 package active dry yeast	Soften yeast in warm water in mixing bowl for 5 minutes. Stir in ¼ cup sugar, salt, 6 tablespoons melted butter, eggs, and sour cream. Gradually add 2¾ to 3 cups flour, beating well after each addition. Cover and let rise in warm place until doubled (about 2 hours). Combine ¾ cup sugar, ¾ cup coconut, and 2 tablespoons orange peel in small bowl; set aside. Knead dough on floured surface about 15 times. Roll out half of dough into 12" circle. Brush with remaining tablespoon of melted butter. Sprinkle with half of coconut mixture. Cut into 12 pie-shaped wedges. Roll each wedge, starting at wide end and rolling to point. Repeat with remaining dough and coconut mixture. Place rolls point-side down in well-greased 9" × 13" pan. Cover and let rise until doubled (about 1 hour). Bake at 350 degrees for 25 to 30 minutes, until golden brown. Combine ingredients for glaze in saucepan and bring to boil. Cook 3 minutes, stirring occasionally. Pour glaze over coffee cake and sprinkle with remaining ½ cup coconut. Cool in pan.
¼ cup warm water	
¼ cup sugar	
1 teaspoon salt	
7 tablespoons melted butter, divided	
2 eggs	
½ cup sour cream	
3 cups all-purpose flour	
¾ cup sugar	
1¼ cup coconut, divided	
2 tablespoons grated orange rind	

GLAZE

¾ cup sugar

½ cup sour cream

2 tablespoons orange juice

¼ cup butter

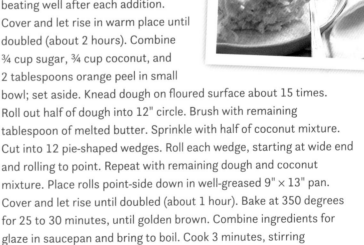

Bringing Spring Indoors

I don't know anyone who isn't ready to celebrate spring after a seemingly endless winter. Bringing natural elements from the outdoors is the most beautiful way to add touches of spring indoors. Here are some easy and affordable ways to do just that:

+ Fill a large galvanized olive bucket with tall cherry blossom branches.

+ Plant a windowsill herb garden.

+ Fill pitchers with aromatic lilacs.

+ Plant greenery and flowers in terra-cotta pots to decorate a mantel.

+ Use bulbs and seed packets decoratively indoors.

+ Search your local antique and thrift shops for botanical prints to frame. (Botanical printables are also available online.) Hang them on walls, or prop them on bookshelves or dressers as a nod to the growing season.

+ Hang a French market basket with fresh or faux flowers on a door or chair back for a casual spring vignette.

+ Display wooden eggs in wire baskets.

+ Lighten up the color palette of the textiles in your home. Simply swapping the throw pillows and blankets can really freshen up a room. Think airy and bright for spring!

TIME TO GET BUSY OUTSIDE

Outdoors, vines now cover the arbors and trellises, and wisteria hangs like nature's bouquets. The grass that has been dormant for months is growing at breakneck speed. It's time to get the riding mower fired up and the vegetable garden planted. And then, when the heavenly smell of lilacs hangs thick in the garden, we are reminded that summer is just around the corner!

I am a big fan of lavender, and dry much of the lavender that grows on our property (above left). Cherries are ripe for the picking from our trees in early summer (above center). Picking blueberries at a local farm is a sweet summer tradition (above right).

Summer

Oh, the long-awaited warmth of summer never comes too soon for us here in the Pacific Northwest! The sunshine feels like medicine after a long stretch of rainy days and dampness. The days are long, with the sun setting after 10 pm in late June. The earth responds with hydrangeas and wildflowers, lavender, and hops. The vegetable garden ramps up to full-production mode, yielding lettuce, tomatoes, zucchini, and cucumbers, to name a few.

THE BEST OF BEING OUTDOORS

During summer, we enjoy going on walks and picking blackberries as we go. We stock up on blueberries at a local blueberry farm, and ride our bikes to get ice cream from a family-owned, all-natural scoop shop that happens to be less than a mile from our house (lucky us!). Our animals also get to take advantage of summer—the dogs enjoy more time playing with our boys since school is out, and we turn the sheep out to graze in larger areas. Even the chickens perk up as they get to take dust baths again and enjoy plenty of sunshine, which is needed for egg production.

To make the most of outdoor living during the summer months, we bring out two picnic tables with benches from the barn and place them in the side pasture, under the trees. To make the evening meals even more enjoyable, we string lights between two tall vintage ladders placed on each side of the tables. We leave this setup for much of the summer and enjoy outdoor meals with family and friends. It is especially nice on extra-warm days to dine under the shade of the trees. (Like many in the Northwest, we don't have air conditioning, and we tend to get "less friendly" when the indoor thermostat holds steady at 85 degrees for days on end!)

SUMMER STAPLES

Summers are for campfires, so I try not to run out of marshmallows, graham crackers, and chocolate. It's usually late afternoon when someone will say, "Can we have a fire tonight?" My husband is almost always game. And usually once or twice a summer, my husband and our boys will pitch a tent in the yard, where they'll sleep beneath the stars. (I enjoy listening through an open window, from the comfort of my own bed.)

SUMMER CHORES

Summer is a good time to tackle certain projects that are easier (or more pleasant) to do when it is dry, such as power washing the fences. Living in the Seattle area, there are certain things we almost always scramble to do before summer ends and the rainy season begins, like moving picnic tables and benches into the barn, cutting back overgrown vines by the house, and cleaning out gutters. No one loves chores, but if you have to do them, do them while the sun is shining! And don't forget your outdoor animals. Summer is the time to deep clean the stalls and chicken coop too.

ENJOYING SUMMER INDOORS

Inside, simplicity works best when school's out and there's lots of activity. In our house, we experience a nearly constant stream of coming in and going out. Sunflowers from the yard, a bowl of fresh fruit, and lavender drying are signs of life inside our summer farmhouse. (Stray sports balls, abandoned water bottles, and lots of kicked-off shoes are other signs of life one will encounter around our house in the summer.) It's always difficult to say goodbye to summer, but the beauty of fall sure helps.

Summer Berry Crisp

SERVES 6

FILLING

5 cups farm-fresh blackberries
   (or frozen berries, thawed and drained)
3 tablespoons sugar
3 tablespoons flour

TOPPING

1 cup regular rolled oats
¾ cup packed light brown sugar
¼ cup all-purpose flour
½ teaspoon ground cinnamon
6 tablespoons salted butter cut into
   small pieces, at room temperature

DIRECTIONS

Preheat oven to 375°. Combine filling ingredients in large bowl, being careful not to smash berries. Divide among six 10-ounce ramekins. In medium bowl, mix together topping ingredients until mixture resembles coarse crumbs. Sprinkle topping, covering blackberries. Place ramekins on baking sheet and bake until topping is golden brown, about 15 to 20 minutes. Serve warm with vanilla ice cream.

Heirloom pumpkins in soft shades are paired with cabbage plants on the porch (above left). Our vintage F-150 provides a rustic backdrop for a tailgate dessert bar (above center). The hops turn golden above our garden gate (above right).

Autumn

The first crisp fall day is so invigorating—a day when the sun is shining, but a sweater still feels like a good idea. The apples are heavy on the trees, just waiting to be picked and enjoyed. The pumpkins in the garden are starting to turn orange, and the leaves are about to put on quite a show. Fall, perhaps the coziest season of all, is here!

INDOOR FALL DECOR

I used to have several tubs of fall decor that I would pull out each fall. However, over the years, I've come to appreciate using fresh or dried natural elements instead. A leafy branch here or there looks beautiful on shelves. Freshly-picked pumpkins stacked in crates, or used as a table centerpiece, provide that farm-fresh fall charm.

One of my favorite things to use for fall decorating is wheat. Wheat has a sun-faded quality and reminds us of the abundance of harvest time. I fill a galvanized bucket or tall basket with wheat for our entry table, or tuck a bundle of wheat stalks in a French market basket and hang it from a door. Wheat is available at craft stores and many home-decorating shops. Or, if (like us) you live near wheat farms, you can call around and see if one of the farms will let you pay to cut a bucket or two full of wheat. It's more economical and can even become a fun little tradition. (I usually bring our boys along to help!)

A benefit of using fresh and dried natural elements for decorating is that there's not as much to store, year-to-year, and very little goes to waste. We feed the pumpkins to our chickens when we're done using them. (See "Chickens Like Pumpkins Too" on page 88.) And the dried wheat can last for multiple seasons.

DON'T FORGET THE PORCH

I really enjoy decorating our porch for fall. I use sun-dried cornstalks to frame the door, and place a vintage orchard ladder stacked with pumpkins in varying faded fall shades. On the door, I hang a dried floral-and-twig wreath, tucking in golden hops vines for added texture and interest. Though I rarely decorate with orange, throw pillows on the bench provide a few fun pops of harvest colors. Vintage cherry buckets are filled with mums and line the porch steps along with . . . you guessed it! More pumpkins.

Chickens Like Pumpkins Too

Leftover pumpkins make great treats for chickens. If they steer clear as if a pumpkin is an unwelcome intruder, cut a small starter hole or slice off a wedge of the pumpkin and place both pieces in their run. As soon as one chicken starts pecking at it, the others will join the party!

BARN PARTY, ANYONE?

If you have a barn, fall is a great season to use it for entertaining. Who doesn't love a rustic barn party? We like to set up tables, benches, and chairs through the center of the barn and hang strings of lights from the ceiling. Straw bales make great alternative seating if you are low on chairs or just want to add more farm charm. Add simple linens (a tablecloth will do!) to make the bales a little less prickly to sit on. Use pumpkins and candles for simple centerpieces and your barn party setting is ready. (If you keep animals in your barn as we do, be sure to clean out stalls just prior to your party to minimize any unpleasant odors.)

Sesame Soy Salmon

SERVES 4–6

INGREDIENTS	DIRECTIONS
1 large salmon fillet (approximately 1.5 pounds) ⅔ cup soy sauce 6 tablespoons minced green onions (include tops) 4 tablespoons sesame oil 2 tablespoons hot chili sesame oil 2 tablespoons rice vinegar 2 tablespoons minced fresh ginger 4 teaspoons sugar 4 cloves minced garlic Dash red pepper	Mix together all ingredients except salmon in medium-sized bowl. Place salmon fillet in large dish, approximately 2" deep. Pour marinade over fillet and cover dish with plastic wrap or foil. Refrigerate for at least 30 minutes up to 3 hours. (The longer it marinates, the more flavorful it will be!) Place salmon fillet on foil-lined baking sheet. Bake at 325° for 45 to 60 minutes, depending on size of fillet and how well done you prefer your salmon. Serve baked salmon over bed of cooked spinach with rice, green salad, and rosemary bread.

*It's a winter wonderland! Snow covers the barn (above left) and farmhouse
(above center), and flocks all the trees. Our sheep weren't quite sure what to
make of their first snow (above right), but were well-prepared in their wool coats.*

Winter

Bare branches and a frost-covered barn set a wintry
scene that greets me as I feed the animals in the
morning. I move a little faster than I did in the fall,
eager to return to the warmth of the house. The
chickens and ducks with their layers of down, and the
sheep with their heavy wool coats, are better suited
for the winter than I am. The sunny wintry mornings
are the best, and the ones with heavy rain are the
worst, as far as feeding rounds go. And then there
are the days, few and far between here in the Pacific
Northwest, when it snows.

*"Winter is a season of
recovery and preparation."*

PAUL THEROUX

LET IT SNOW!

Snow days here at our little farmstead are nothing
short of magical, as we see the world through the
eyes of our hat-and-scarf-clad children. And our
dogs. (I think snow is our dogs' version of Disneyland.
They roll in it, jump in it, race in it—it's entertaining to
watch!) In our area of the country, where there isn't
much heavy snow-removal equipment, even an inch
or two of snow is all it takes for schools to quickly
shut down. Grocery store shelves will be emptied at
near-apocalyptic speed. And there is a general sense
of giddiness mixed with pride in survivorship, as we
take the kids sledding and then warm up with hot
chocolate, tuning in to storm-watch updates on the
local news.

*A bright and airy
white backdrop mixed
with weathered wood
furniture and accessories
is one of my favorite
interior combinations.
A minimally decorated
space can add to a sense
of peace and tranquility
in the home.*

WINTER ON THE INSIDE

Indoors, we love decking our halls for the holidays. (See "Farmhouse Christmas" on page 99.) After the holidays, I enjoy the fresh, clean, minimal slate that comes once the Christmas decorations are taken down. I like to bring in more plants and will sometimes wind a strand of cafe lights around a vintage orchard ladder to bring more light into our rainy and gray Seattle winter days.

Apart from the hustle and bustle of Christmas (the star of winter!) and the excitement of an occasional snow, winter is a more reflective season. There's a natural break from the pressure of yard work. The days are shorter, and more time is spent indoors. (For us, "indoors" is a mix of spending time in the house and in the school basketball gym cheering on our boys.) After the holidays, my thoughts tend to turn toward planning the garden, spring projects, and summer adventures.

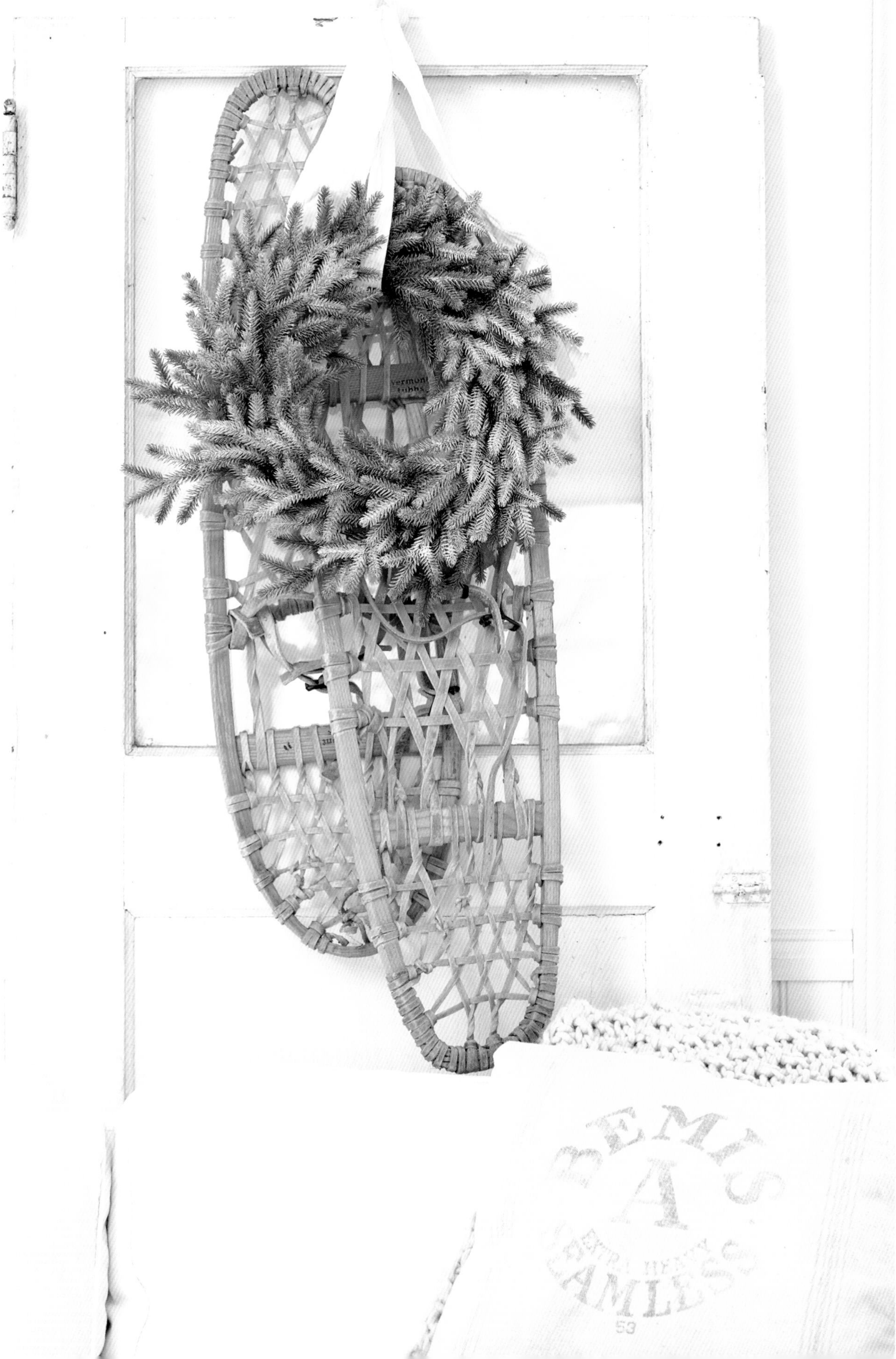
BEMIS
A

Butternut Squash and Sausage Risotto

Adapted from *All Things New* by Kelly Minter

SERVES 8

INGREDIENTS

16 ounces arborio rice

1 pound loose pork sausage
(if cased, remove
from casing)

3 to 4 cups cubed butternut
squash (precut squash
is more expensive, but
saves a lot of time!)

1 tablespoon olive oil

½ onion, diced
(about ½ cup)

6 cups chicken broth

⅔ cup white wine

2 tablespoons butter
(or olive oil)

½ cup shaved or grated
parmesan cheese

DIRECTIONS

Preheat oven to 425°. Place cubed butternut squash on foil-lined baking sheet (for easy cleanup). Drizzle with olive oil, and season with salt and pepper. Bake until edges are lightly browned, approximately 20 to 25 minutes. While squash is roasting, cook ground sausage in Dutch oven or large pan, stirring to break up sausage.

Drain most of fat, but keep small amount in Dutch oven or pan for flavor. Set aside cooked sausage in bowl. Using same Dutch oven or pan, sauté onion with 2 tablespoons butter or olive oil on medium heat for 3 minutes. Add rice and stir until well coated, about 2 minutes. Add wine and cook for another minute, letting strong wine flavor burn off. Add one cup of broth, stirring continually until broth is absorbed. Repeat with each remaining cup of broth, waiting until current broth is absorbed before adding another. If it seems like you can still add more liquid after 6 cups of broth, add ½ cup of water or broth until rice is soft and creamy (not crunchy), and to your liking. After rice is cooked, add butternut squash, sausage, and parmesan to Dutch oven or pan, stirring gently to avoid smashing squash. Salt and pepper to taste. Serve with a green vegetable like asparagus.

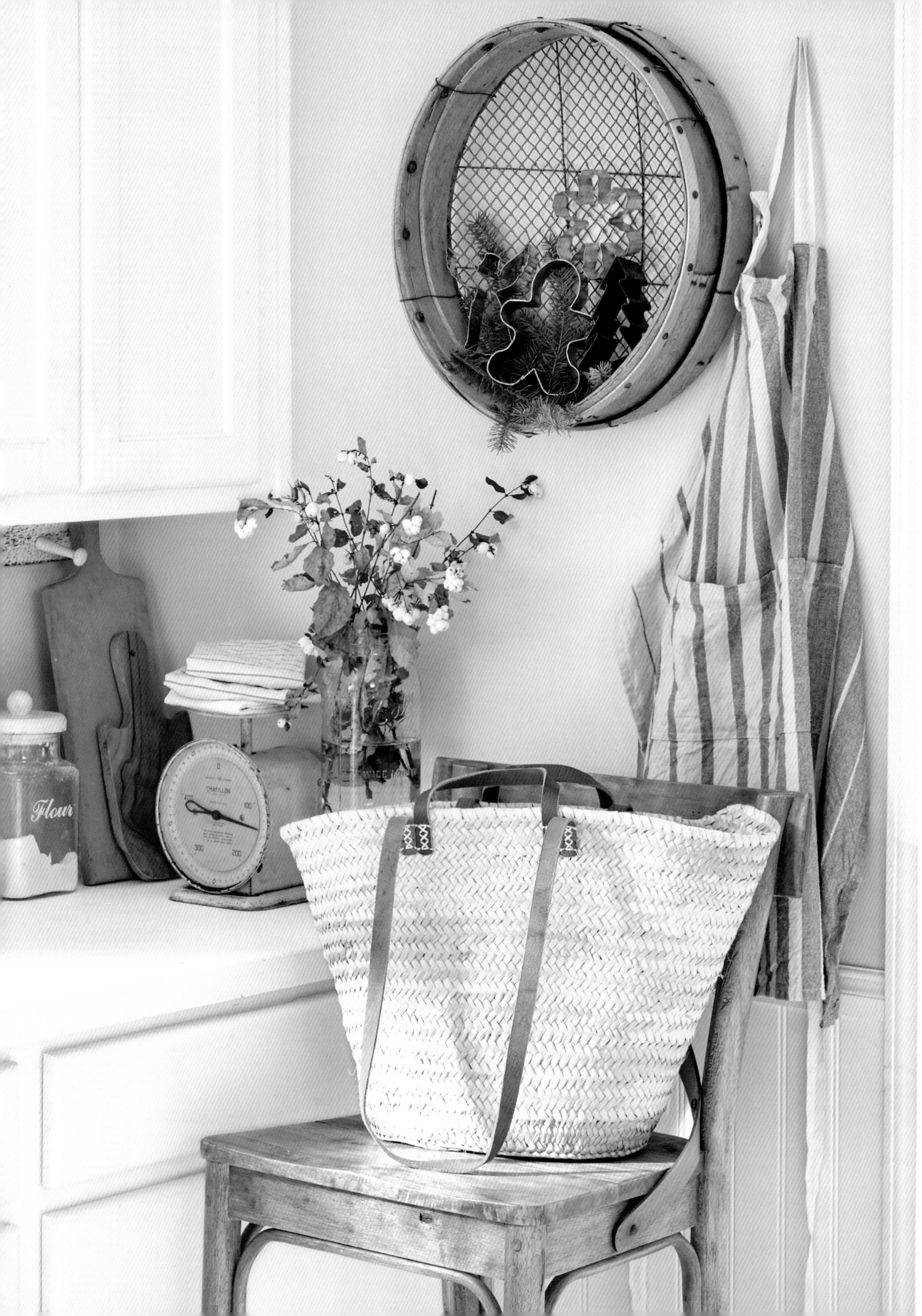
Flour
CHATILLON
400
100
300
200

CHAPTER 6

Farmhouse Christmas

"Our hearts grow tender with childhood memories and love of kindred, and we are better throughout the year for having, in spirit, become a child again at Christmastime."

LAURA INGALLS WILDER

Years ago, when we were house hunting, one of the questions I would think about was, "Can I picture this house at Christmastime?" It became my benchmark question. Where would we put the tree? How would the house look decorated? Could we visualize it? And would Norman Rockwell approve? OK, we'll never know the answer to that last question, but let's just say that Christmas has always been important to my family and me. It truly is the most wonderful time of the year!

Christmas for All Your Senses

To create a special holiday backdrop, think about engaging all five of your senses in your home over the Christmas season. Here are some of my favorite ways to do that:

SIGHT. Picture the sparkling lights of a Christmas tree. (For me, that's sparkling as in continuous white lights, not flashing. Flashing lights make me anxious! Just a personal preference.) Words can also be used as a visual reminder of the reason we celebrate; a large scroll with lyrics from a favorite Christmas carol hangs over the living room mantel (see page 100).

SOUND. Many memories center around favorite Christmas carols. Christmas music is such a joyful, celebratory soundtrack at home. I also think of classic Christmas movies and how nice it is to have one playing in the background, even at times when you can't necessarily sit down and watch a whole movie.

A warm, festive atmosphere is the goal of Christmas decorating in our home. The living room Christmas tree is laden with precious family memories.

SMELL. The aromas of a fresh-cut pine tree, sugar cookies baking, and favorite winter candles all add to the scents of the season.

TASTE. Back to those cookies . . . sugar, gingerbread, shortbread . . . we've yet to encounter one we didn't like! I have a collection of vintage Santa mugs that our kids enjoy drinking hot chocolate from or using to make "Santa sundaes" (peppermint ice cream, hot fudge, and whipped cream).

TOUCH. 'Tis the season for chunky blankets, hats, and scarves! I like to keep a basket of warm blankets in our family room, and often hang blankets from a vintage ladder in the living room. Sweater (knit) pillows and grain-sack pillows provide added warmth and texture this time of year as well.

Tree Hunting

One of our first family traditions of the season is going tree hunting in the mountains. In Washington state, tree permits cost five dollars per tree, and each family is allowed up to five trees. It's a great excuse to spend the day adventuring out in the forest together! We used to use only real trees, but now enjoy a combination of real mixed with some snow-covered faux trees. I enjoy leaving some trees bare for a simple, natural feel. But we always decorate the tree in our living room (page 100) with our family's collection of ornaments. It's like unearthing a time capsule as we unwrap ornaments gifted to us by family and friends, and others from vacations and places we've traveled. Picture ornaments bring smiles all around, and of course giggles erupt at some of the ornaments our sons crafted over the years, with lots of heart—and lots of glue!

Christmas Traditions for Kids

When you have children, it's fun to start traditions that incorporate them and their starry-eyed wonder for Christmas.

ADVENT CALENDAR

One custom we enjoy is hanging numbered little white buckets from the chicken nesting boxes in the family room. Our one-of-a-kind advent calendar holds treats or small toys each day in December until Christmas. The younger the children, the more excited they'll be to rush downstairs to see what awaits each day. Older kids are in less of a hurry, but they still enjoy the special treats!

CHRISTMAS BOOKS

Another go-to Christmas tradition is displaying children's Christmas books in a wooden crate on our coffee table. These are books we've collected over the years. From my favorite childhood Christmas book (*Santa Mouse*) to *Polar Express, The Night Before Christmas,* and Nativity books, each one is a memory. I hope that one day when our children are grown they will see these books and think of their childhood Christmases with renewed joy and wonder.

HUNTING FOR CHRISTMAS TREES

Spending a day in nature, walking through the woods in the nearby mountains to choose just the right Christmas trees, has become a fun adventure for our family. The five of us head out in the truck, stop at a coffee stand for something warm to drink, and enjoy the wintry, mountain scenery while listening to Christmas music.

CHRISTMAS EVE CANDLELIGHT SERVICE

Each Christmas Eve, after enjoying dinner with family, we head to church for a special candlelight service. We sing carols while string instruments play, and hold candles that represent Jesus, the light of the world. It's a cherished time, as I look down the row of seats and see my husband and our children along with cousins, grandparents, and an aunt and uncle.

Decorating for the Season

Christmas decorating is not a one-day event at our house. It is usually completed over the course of a few weeks when we have windows of time in our busy schedule.

Amid the joy and nostalgia, there is usually a point in the middle of decorating where things look more undone than done, and for a moment I think, "I can't live like this!" But as the saying goes, "It's darkest before the dawn"; it also seems to be true that it's messy before it's merry! When the house is finally decorated and cleaned, a bell rings and an angel gets its wings . . . or at least that's what it feels like should happen!

GIFT WRAPPING THE HOUSE

One of the most fun places to decorate for Christmas is the porch. It's kind of like the gift wrapping of the house—it's the first thing people see! It doesn't need to be overdone to be festive. I enjoy using a few wintry, snow day–inspired things like a sled, ice skates, and boots. Firewood in a wheelbarrow and mini trees in galvanized containers provide a rustic, more-natural-than-commercial, welcoming feeling. A wreath and scarf dress up the doorway, giving it an easy, celebratory sense.

TIME-WORN TREASURES

I enjoy incorporating timeworn treasures into our holiday decor. A large antique European dough bowl holds gifts under the tree. Little stacks of old books can be found tucked around the house, holding candles or vintage ornaments. And speaking of vintage ornaments, I especially appreciate the ones in their original packaging. I imagine how things might have been back in the 1940s and 1950s, when these same ornament packages were taken out to decorate. I'm reminded how much joy there is in the preparation for, and anticipation of, Christmas.

*A beautiful tablescape
does not need to be
expensive. I found
the brass candlestick
holders at a thrift store
and bought the seeded
eucalyptus and
pomegranates at a
local grocery store.*

BEYOND THE LIVING ROOMS

In the dining room, we place one of the imperfect, yet beautiful, trees we brought
back from the mountains. The table is decorated simply, with a European grain sack
runner, seeded eucalyptus sprigs, pomegranates, and candles. We found the fun
"Merry & Bright" handmade sign on the mantel at a charming vintage co-op in
Coeur d'Alene, Idaho, while visiting family for Thanksgiving.

*During the Christmas season, vintage Santa mugs and mid-century milkglass
Tom and Jerry cups are hung from the French drying rack, which our kids interpret
as an invitation for hot chocolate or a "Santa sundae." Greenery and a few bottle
brushes shaped like trees on the windowsills add to a festive feeling in the kitchen.*

A few cheery Christmas touches in the kitchen and bedrooms carries the magic of the season throughout the house. Our children each have a small Christmas tree in their rooms, with their own little collection of ornaments. We let them pick out one ornament a year to add to their tree.

Even a wrapping station can be both decorative and functional when made into a little vignette. I corral rolls of wrapping paper into an antique water bucket. I have a weakness for French bistro chairs, and recently found a weathered red one, which works perfectly as part of this holiday spot.

While Christmas decorations have regularly been a part of our children's rooms, I've recently begun to add a few Christmas accents in our master bedroom. If you've never decorated bedrooms for Christmas, I'd encourage you to try just a few merry accessories. I think you'll be surprised by the joyful mood they help create.

I hang a couple of knit stockings from our headboard (above), and replace the neutral blanket at the foot of the bed with a red plaid blanket with (faux) fur detail. A vintage European red-striped grain-sack pillow also provides a timeless nod to the season.

It's Christmas Outdoors Too

Having outbuildings on the property provides more of a canvas to decorate! It doesn't cost much to add some creative, festive touches to the chicken coop, which is visited daily when we feed the chickens and ducks. Mini stockings and a tree from the mountains add to the merriment outdoors.

The barn is another fun place to incorporate some Christmas cheer. Last year, we hosted family here for a Christmas Eve dinner. It was one of the few years that it actually snowed on Christmas Eve and Christmas Day! After dinner inside, we crunched through the snow to a festively decorated barn, where we enjoyed a Christmas dessert together (among the hum of the space heaters!). After dessert, we all headed to church, as we do each year, for the candlelight Christmas Eve service.

To All a Good Night

Returning home after Christmas Eve service, we give our boys one gift and they eventually go to sleep. The next morning comes early (though not *as* early as when they were younger!). Racing down the stairs, they hurry to see what is under the tree. It's such a happy time. We'll always cherish these memories in our hearts.

Farmhouse Christmas

CHAPTER 7

Farmhouse Gatherings

"Homes are happiest when they are being used."

MYQUILLYN SMITH

One of our dreams when we were house hunting was to find a place where we could spend time with family and friends outside as well as indoors—a place where we could enjoy nature together. We are thankful to now have such a space where guests can feel relaxed and comfortable. When we have friends over in the summer, we almost always eat outdoors. (In Seattle, you learn to take advantage of sunshine whenever possible!) Usually, the food includes something grilled, a seasonal salad, and a berry fruit crisp with ice cream. Having property has been so nice because it allows the adults to linger around the table while the kids take off to play games with plenty of space to themselves. As the weather cools, a barn makes it possible to extend the outdoor entertaining season.

Setting the Stage

When hosting a special meal, I think about the setting and consider a backdrop or focal point. Usually, when eating outdoors, the backdrop is simply the beautiful maple trees in our side yard. But sometimes it's fun to do a little something extra.

Once we used our old pickup truck as a flower stand. I filled several containers with flowers from our yard and my parents' yard, and bought a few bouquets from the farmers' market. (Fortunately, many flower growers dot the landscape nearby, and they sell at all the local farmers' markets at very reasonable prices.) I already owned a large painted

vintage "flowers" sign, which I propped against the truck. This rustic flower stand served as a backdrop for dinner and for pictures. At the end of the night, for favors, we invited our guests to choose Mason jars with flowers of their choice. It was a special summer evening, celebrating close friends who were moving back to England. Our group picture, taken in front of the flower truck, was a sentimental going-away gift.

Farm-Fresh Favors

Sending guests home with a little taste of the country is a thoughtful way to thank them for coming. At each table setting, place favors that will double as table decor. Include a name or initial, and they do triple duty as place cards. The possibilities are endless, but depending on the season and occasion, here are some ideas for things you may enjoy giving:

+ Small bundles of dried lavender tied with a ribbon or twine

+ Wooden berry baskets filled with seasonal berries

+ Blackberry jam in Mason jars (blackberries run rampant in our area, so it's easy and free to pick gallons to make your own jam)

+ Mini loaves of pumpkin bread, baked in purchased cardboard loaf pans

+ Candles with a farmhouse scent (vanilla, lavender, apple, pumpkin, spice, etc.)

+ Monogrammed mugs tied with sprigs of greenery

+ Miniature herb gardens in terra-cotta pots

+ A half dozen farm-fresh eggs with a personalized label or stamp

Creating an Outdoor Eating Area

Everyone's property is laid out differently, but here are some tips to help you plan an outdoor dining space where you live.

Determine a location. Asking the following questions may help:

+ Do you have an existing deck you could use?

+ Is there a beautiful setting on your property you'd like to take advantage of?

+ Is the area convenient for accessing the kitchen or grill for food and drinks?

+ Is there shade, or could you provide shade with umbrellas?

Set up sturdy tables and chairs or benches that can withstand the heat and even some rain (depending on your location) so that you can leave them out during the summer season if possible. If you have to put furniture away after every meal, you'll be less enthusiastic to set it all up again.

Adding lighting, such as string lights, allows your meals or parties to comfortably (and beautifully!) extend past dark. Often you can hang string lights from surrounding posts or trees. However, if (like us) you need to bring in your own posts to attach the string lights to, consider using two tall wooden ladders on either end of the length of your table(s). You'll want to use a lightweight string light such as globe lights. (Avoid the heavier, commercial string lights, since the weight of those strands can actually cause your ladders to collapse forward. Ask me how I know!) Other layers of lighting might include candlelit lanterns on the table or a pathway of luminarias.

Use linens and textiles to make your eating area comfortable and stylish. Bring tablecloths, linen napkins, pillows, or throw blankets inside after using so they won't fade in the sun.

Keep drinks cold in a large galvanized tub filled with ice.

Dress up your space with farm-fresh flowers.

Create a fire pit close by (if space permits), complete with additional seating where post-dinner s'mores can be enjoyed.

Heading to the Barn

When the seasons change and we're no longer able to eat outdoors, entertaining moves back to the house, and sometimes even into the barn. You might think of a barn as a casual place, but with some fun decor, you can dress it up as much as you like.

We've used our barn for social events for the boys and their friends, but we've also held family gatherings there, including Thanksgiving dinner. To add extra seating, have some straw bales on hand, and simply place a linen or blanket on top. I also like to use mismatched chairs for a casual, interesting atmosphere. In lieu of tablecloths, choose an antique blanket or quilt for your table topper, adding character and historic charm that's especially fitting for Thanksgiving.

Extra lighting can be necessary in a big barn, so we hang string lights and use candles on the tables for a warm glow. If it's especially chilly, bring in a couple of space heaters and consider placing a pair of knitted gloves at each place for an unexpected but practical favor.

An 1800s chippy farmhouse mantel creates a pretty focal point at the back of the barn. I added pumpkins and an oversized grapevine wreath embellished with colorful leafy branches from our yard. The table is set with my dad's antique woven coverlet as the attractive base layer.

Near Christmas, I enjoy having a group of girlfriends over for lunch, before our kids are out of school for winter break. It's always so nice to catch up in person and savor the holiday season over a cup (or more!) of coffee. With Christmas decorations up, and Christmas music playing in the background, it's bound to be a joyful little soiree. While we enjoy lunch in the dining room, sometimes it adds to the fun to visit our Babydoll sheep in the decorated-for-Christmas barn afterward. (I'm beginning to wonder if some of my friends come to see us or Teddy, Winston, and George!) This past year we even took pictures with the sheep, and my dear friends with the amazing shoes got right in the stall with the rest of us!

Birthdays Are Bigger in the Country

Some of our most special memories here at our little farmstead have been our boys' birthday parties and playtimes with friends. Having extra space in the yard has provided a lot of fun options we didn't have before. I remember the first year we lived here, our youngest son had a Cowboys and Indians themed birthday party. Our neighbor brought her horse over and took the kids for rides in our riding arena.

Then there was the year our middle son had about twenty friends over to play laser tag! And we'll always remember our oldest son and his teenage friends having dinner in the barn with a tailgate-style party, followed by a campfire outside. (See page 127 for more details on hosting your own tailgate party.)

A few years ago, my husband turned the barn's hayloft into a rustic home-movie theater. (My contribution was finding 12 antique theater seats.) Our sons have had fun watching movies and basketball games there, together and with friends. Since we didn't need the hayloft to store large amounts of hay, it was the perfect space to repurpose for our kids to use and enjoy.

Having some pastureland makes a perfect spot for outdoor events. At times we've turned ours into a homemade baseball field for a vintage-baseball birthday party. The boys have pitched a tent there for a summer sleepover. We've even had an entire soccer team make use of our pasture when our youngest son's team couldn't find a good field for practices. When you have a bit of open space, you soon learn that your backyard can become the place to be. And that's something we just love about living on a little farmstead. When our kids want to have friends over and we see them turn off the video games and head outdoors, it's a wonderful thing!

At a baseball-themed birthday party, guests helped themselves to hot dogs, potato chips, watermelon, and soda at the "concession stand" (above left). A special father/son moment at our then five-year-old's Cowboys and Indians birthday party (above right).

Setting Up a Tailgate Party

We have a 1976 Ford F-150 truck and love using it for tailgate parties. If you don't have a truck, you can do the same on and around a picnic table. The key for an eye-catching tailgate backdrop is to include rustic items of varying heights.

Start with large stackable surfaces, like straw bales, tables, or a truck bed. You can purchase a straw bale for about $12 at your local feed shop. If you're using a truck, load a bale in the back—it will serve as the highest point of your setup. If you're using a table, angle a straw bale or trunk in front of one corner of your serving table to provide dimension and more of that rustic, fall feeling.

Gather galvanized buckets and wood crates for farm-style serving pieces. We use a galvanized tub filled with ice for drinks, and an antique crate is a perfect serving tray for caramel apples. Turn another crate over to use as a stand for a tray stacked with sandwiches, sliders, or hot dogs.

Bring in a plaid or wool game-day blanket or two that you can drape off the side of the table or hay bale or over the back of the tailgate. It warms up the scene and adds another layer of texture.

Use fun, interesting accents like vintage thermoses or sports pennants.

Add natural finishing touches that give a nod to the fall season, such as pumpkins and wheat. It's even more fun if the pumpkins are ones your family grew themselves!

Last, but not least, light it up! Use string lights above your backdrop to bring cheer to your party and take your gathering from day to night. Use a lightbox (sold at craft stores as well as online) as a fun, personalized sign.

Autumn Alfresco Dining

Early fall, while it's still sunny and warm and the leaves are beginning to change color, is the perfect time to enjoy alfresco dining in the country. If your garden is still blooming, gather flowers from your yard, or pick up some beautiful flower bouquets at a local farmers' market. We used dahlias in shades of orange and red, and golden-yellow black-eyed Susans. A fresh persimmon adds a charming touch to each place setting.

Items to Keep On Hand for Gatherings

When it comes to indoor/outdoor entertaining, you may want to make each event sparkle on its own, with unique table settings, favors, and more. But it's good to have all the basics on hand that you can use over and over again, regardless of the party's theme or the crowd you're hosting.

+ Tables and benches or chairs. Consider sturdy, picnic-style tables and benches and/or mix-and-match style chairs.

+ Large beverage dispenser (clear glass allows creative or colorful drinks to be seen).

+ Galvanized buckets for chilling drinks, farmhouse-style flower arrangements, etc.

+ Crates of varying sizes to stack plates in, use as stands, or serve food items like wrapped sandwiches or bags of chips.

+ Table linens, including tablecloths, runners, and napkins.

+ Easy, sturdy drinking glasses like Mason jars and enamelware.

CHAPTER 8

Farmhouse Finds

" It doesn't take money to have style,
it just takes a really good eye. "

Tyler Florence

"Where do you shop for your home?" is a question I'm sometimes asked. There's usually an awkward pause while I search for an uncomplicated response. In short, I shop almost everywhere. From favorite antique shops to yard sales, online marketplaces (Craigslist, Facebook Marketplace, OfferUp, etc.), home-goods stores, thrift stores, local boutiques, and vintage markets, I shop them all. And please be careful if you happen to be driving behind me; I've been known to make sudden stops for roadside rescues. (We've brought home at least three curbside tables . . . and two were really cute!)

In short, you have a lot of great options when it comes to shopping for farmhouse decor. And many are right at your fingertips.

Online Marketplaces

Believe it or not, we found our nineteenth-century Swedish Mora clock through Craigslist. It was still an investment, but it is a unique piece that is hard to come by, especially in our price range. We've found some of our highest-quality pieces at affordable prices through various online marketplaces. In addition, we've even been given several really nice things, like a vintage art table and an antique iron daybed, by people who just wanted to clear out some space in their homes. There are certain keywords I use to regularly search for items, including *antique*, *vintage*, *rustic*, *French*, *shabby*, *chippy*, *farm*, *farmhouse*, *wood*, and *paint*. But now that I've given you my secret, be sure to leave a few good finds for me!

skate a(e)

In all seriousness, when buying and selling through online channels, it is important to be cautious since often you don't really know who you are dealing with. Some of the marketplace sites now include buyer and seller ratings, which are based on reviews. Many vendors are willing to meet in a neutral, public place, which helps alleviate personal safety concerns.

Antique Shops

A great destination for finding one-of-a-kind pieces is an antique shop. I've had the most shopping success at stores that have many different vendors (providing a varied selection of items), and usually at shops that are located in a more affordable area of town (which is reflected in more reasonable prices!).

Two years ago, I began renting a space to sell some of my own vintage finds in one of my favorite local antique shops—M&M Antiques in Monroe, Washington. I enjoy interacting with people who share a love for timeworn and well-loved things.

A benefit of this type of arrangement is that the owners of the shop provide day-to-day sales coverage, so I just have to make time to restock, refresh, and rearrange as needed.

Vintage Markets and Shows

I'll never forget the first time I went to the Farm Chicks Antiques Show in Spokane, Washington. This show is a farmhouse lover's dream! They sell everything from authentic farm supplies, like chicken waterers, farm signs, vintage bulb crates, and even windmills, to pillows made from grain sacks and wool army blankets. Chippy furniture and creative, handmade decor overflows! Just taking in the show and how the vendors display items provides so much inspiration to bring back home.

PLEASE DO NOT CUT
BAG WHEN OPENING

THIS BAG SHOULD BE
RETURNED TO

Peoples
National Bank
of Washington

What to Look for When Antiquing

Often antique shops will be filled to the brim. And while some people like to "dig" for treasures, others can be put off by the sheer volume of merchandise and don't know where to start. Here are a few ideas to consider before heading out on your next antiquing adventure:

+ Think about items that can help you personalize your space. For example, my work involves home decorating, which often includes painting. I'm drawn to sturdy old paint brushes that show signs of use. I've hung them on a wall as artwork in my home office space.

+ Search for beautiful and useful storage options. A collection of antique blue Mason jars of varying sizes and ages provides a pop of color and is useful for storing small household items. Old baskets, which bring wood tones and an artisan feel to the home, are another example

of an aesthetically pleasing storage option. (Baskets are perfect for storing throw blankets and pillows.)

+ Freshen up your home with a fun seasonal antique in your entryway or on the porch. In summer, an antique croquet set adds a happy and carefree feeling. In the winter, a pair of old ice skates will bring a touch of whimsy.

+ Personalize gift giving with antiques: a beautiful antique cake stand for a mom who loves to bake, a galvanized watering can for a friend who is right at home in the garden, or a special antique book for someone who loves to read. Even children have shown an appreciation for their own little piece of history—like a corn-husk doll, Native American hunting bow, or old leather football.

Another show I enjoy attending is The Great Junk Hunt. The organization behind this event holds shows in various cities, so look them up online to see if there is one near you. In my area, they have two shows a year; my favorite one is in November because it is filled with charming vintage holiday decor. It's such a fun way to kick off the Christmas season—treasure hunting with family or friends while musicians play Christmas music in the background.

Don't forget to check out local markets when you travel. Years ago, I had the opportunity to explore the many stalls at the Paris Flea Market, and last summer, our family spent the day at the world's largest antique market (over 1,000 vendors!), the Portobello Market in London. You may not be able to ship large furniture pieces home, but it's fun to look for treasures that are small enough to fit in your suitcase. You'll remember your trip each time you spy that one-of-a-kind piece on your mantel or bookshelf.

Yard, Barn, and Garage Sales

During the summer months, I keep my eyes out for yard, barn, and garage-sale signs. Usually prices are low, and you can find some great deals on unique items. Our kids have gotten used to stopping at sales with me. One of my boys likes to alert me to the signs, saying, "Hey Mom! There's a garage sale!" while one of his brothers quickly shushes him. (The mood of the car is greatly benefited if my boys are on the lookout for something themselves, like sports cards!) Patience and perseverance are key when garage "sale-ing"—I will often hit three or four flops before scoring big. (Let's chalk it up to the thrill of the hunt!) And when bartering, I try to be polite, and ask, "Are you flexible at all on that price?" You never know until you ask . . . .

Tips for Shopping at Markets and Shows

A friend who had recently gone to her first vintage market described feeling overwhelmed by all the options. I remember that feeling too. You can easily overspend, or go the other way and leave empty-handed because you can't decide. Here are a few tips to help you shop smart:

+ Decide on a budget, and then take cash in the amount you intend to spend. It's easy to overspend with a credit card if you're not careful or disciplined. Also, sometimes vendors only accept cash or they're more willing to bargain with a shopper who is paying cash.

+ Narrow down what you are looking for and write a list to take with you. Are you decorating for an upcoming holiday or hosting a special occasion? Perhaps you're looking for a gift or two? Or are you in the market for a piece of furniture or a few accessories to put on a new entry table? Stick to your list.

+ Bring a large tote, market basket, or cart (if permitted in the venue) to comfortably carry your finds.

+ Bring a bottle of water so that you don't have to spend your time waiting in line at a concession stand.

+ If you find something you love, don't assume it will be there later. If you love it, someone else probably will too. Be prepared to make a decision in the moment or you may miss out.

+ Many shows offer both vintage and new items. In general, vintage items are harder to find, so I prioritize shopping for them. At times it can be hard to tell at a glance, as there are very good reproductions these days. It's OK to ask.

Vintage Quilts

I love the artistry of vintage quilts. Imagining the effort someone put into making a quilt not only functional, but also beautiful, warms my heart. The aqua quilt (above left) came from M&M Antiques, and the multicolored quilt in the basket (above right) has a special story. I saw it at a vintage sale when we were trying to purchase our little farmstead. Our contingent offer was about to expire, and we had no serious buyers for our existing house. I thought the quilt would be perfect for what I hoped would soon be our farmhouse and decided to buy it, in faith that the sale would go through. I'm glad I did, and thankful it all worked out. A month after I bought the quilt, we received an offer!

Thrift Stores

I have a cyclical relationship with thrift stores. I tend to go through long stretches where I don't shop from them, and then I'm back at buzzing them every few weeks or so. My best thrift-store trophies have been our farmhouse dining table (it just needed some paint and a little TLC) and a vintage wood coffee table.

When thrift-store shopping, I've learned to take an extra minute or two to really look over an item to determine its value. I remember when I spotted a silverware chest at a thrift store and assumed it would be empty or contain a cheap set of silverware. I'm glad I took the time to open the box, because inside was a beautiful set of gold-plated flatware, with a value far above the $17 price tag.

Home Stores and More

With farmhouse-style decorating experiencing mainstream appeal, many home stores now carry furniture, decor, and essentials fitting a country home.

Small local businesses offer a personal touch. Often, specialty items are available that may typically be found online, providing customers with savings on shipping costs.

That said, shopping online makes products from all over the world accessible. I've purchased some of my favorite farmhouse basics, like linen towels and European grain sacks, online. And we happily offer farmhouse finds on our own online shop at LittleFarmstead.com.

My home work area incorporates finds from a variety of places. The vintage blue Mason jars were mostly purchased at yard sales. The old paint brushes and work apron I bought at a vintage market. The cattle scroll was purchased online. The wood file came from a thrift store, and many of the other items were bought at home stores.

LITTLE FARMSTEAD LIVING

I think people are drawn to country living for many reasons and in many seasons of their lives. The desire to live closer to nature, a love of animals, a passion for gardening, and the appeal of privacy and serenity are a few reasons that come to mind. Young people may embrace a homesteading way of life as an antidote to a fast-paced, high-tech world. Later in life, people may look to life in the country with nostalgia and want to return to a simpler, slower lifestyle. And for those raising a family, they may dream of a generational home where their children can have room to roam like they did as kids.

As I was writing this book, I reflected over the five years we've made this little farmstead our home. Has it been all that we imagined it would be? Without hesitation, I can say yes—and then some. There's a Miranda Lambert song called, "The House That Built Me." It tells of going back to her childhood home to visit: "Out here it's like I'm someone else, I thought that maybe I could find myself . . . Won't take nothing but a memory from the house that built me." I can't help but think of our three sons playing in the yard with our dogs, climbing fences to pick blackberries, and throwing a football with their papa in the yard. To us, our little farmstead is more than a house, more than a parcel of land. We've planted roots here and made so many memories. This place has given us more reasons to be at home together.

I think back to that Christmas morning when our youngest son unwrapped a replica rifle and Davy Crockett outfit. He spent the day hiding behind every large rock on our property, toy rifle in hand, and we'd see his coonskin hat pop up while he looked for bears!

And then there's our middle son, who has always had a way with birds. You need to catch a chicken? I know who to call. How he begged us for a duck, and we finally gave in. Seeing those little ducklings following our boys around the house that spring was pretty cute, I have to admit.

I think of how, nearly every time we get home from being out and about, our oldest son announces, "I'm going to take the dogs out." He grew up under those big maple trees, walking around with those Labs by his side.

And I remember just how dark it felt at night when we first moved in, and how brightly the stars shone. I think of the special times we've shared here together with family and friends, the joy of growing our own vegetables and the satisfaction of farm-fresh eggs.

Over the years, people have written me, sharing their similar hopes and dreams of embracing a country lifestyle. I wish them wide open spaces too, when the time is just right for them. And when it is, I recommend they invest in boots, ladders, and a riding mower.

It's not *all* butterflies and roses. It's a lot of work trying to keep up with a house, property, and outbuildings while raising a family. Sometimes it can be overwhelming. Even now if I think about it, my mind wanders to how badly the fences could use a power wash and how overgrown the flowerbeds have become.

Still, with all there is to do, the joy of living here is never lost on my husband or me. Living on a little farmstead is what we wanted, craved, dreamed of, and prayed for. We are so very thankful. *It's been a dream come true.*

~ *Julie Thomas*

Acknowledgments

This book is a dream come true. It was a real collaboration, and as such, there are many I'd like to thank.

First, thank you God! Everything I have is from You, and belongs to You. There is no sweeter friend. Thank you for never leaving my side. My prayer is that Your fingerprints will be evident throughout our lives, as well as in these pages.

To my amazing husband, Aaron, thank you for your love and encouragement. The first time I saw you smile it felt like home, and it still does today. . . *more than ever.* Your strength and humor brighten every day. I'm so grateful it's you by my side! Thank you for working so hard to make our dreams come true. I love you!

To my precious children, Hudson, Noah, and Lincoln, you give me that "Christmas came early!" feeling throughout the year. You have filled my life, and our home, with so much joy. I pray you always carry your childhood in your hearts, knowing how deeply you are cherished. (And when you hear the song "Cotton Fields," I hope you'll think of our family with a smile.) Thank you for being such great sports through the writing of this book—putting on pants and nice shirts when you'd rather have stayed in shorts. I love you with all my heart!

I'm forever grateful to my parents for your selfless love and support. Mom, you are not only the wind beneath my wings, but the tornado as well (in all the best ways!). For being my sounding board, helping with the boys, praying, and the many additional ways you assisted in making this book happen, thank you so much! Dad, thank you for always being a source of wisdom and encouragement, for taking the boys to practices, and always covering our family in prayers.

To my sister, Jodi, thank you for helping us search for just the right home for all those years (long before you became a realtor!), and for all the memorable times we've shared home staging, stocking our vintage booths, and raising our children together. Lance, Luke, Jack, and Julia— I'm so proud to call you family. Thank you for being a part of this book.

Thank you to my mother-in-law and father-in-law for raising such a wonderful son, for happy times together at your home in the country, and for sharing Buster with us.

My heartfelt thanks to my dear friends who have walked with us through many seasons of life and have encouraged me while writing this book.

To all the wonderful people at Martingale who have made this book-publishing process such a positive and memorable experience, thank you! Jennifer and Karen, I'm so grateful you believed in our story and took a chance on us. (Karen, I will never forget meeting at the cafe and reviewing edits as Seattle's 2019 Snowmageddon began outside the window!) Adrienne, I'm so appreciative for your creative eye, design expertise, and your desire to stay true to the vision of this book. Adam and Brent, you captured such beautiful images and brought these pages to life. Thank you.

ABOUT THE AUTHOR

Julie Thomas authors the home-decor and lifestyle blog Little Farmstead. Her design work has been featured in magazines and online in the United States and Europe. With a background in home staging and redesign, she finds joy in creating warm and welcoming spaces for living. Having an appreciation for both American and European farmhouse style, Julie enjoys searching for time-worn treasures as a vintage and antiques dealer. Upon earning her Business degree, she honed her writing skills by working on marketing campaigns in the technology sector. Later, her job in the aerospace industry gave her the opportunity to travel, learn about different cultures, and observe design aesthetics throughout the world. Julie grew up in California, and has lived in the Pacific Northwest for eighteen years. She treasures everyday life with her husband, three sons, and a menagerie of animals on their family's mini farm, just past the city limits.

Follow Julie at LittleFarmstead.com, and on social media at:

Instagram.com/littlefarmstead

Facebook.com/littlefarmstead